HALLOWEEN IN AMERICA

A COLLECTOR'S GUIDE WITH PRICES

Pick A Pumpkin and on its back You'll find your future bright or black

2nd Edition

Stuart Schneider

Schiffer Publishing Ltd

77 Lower Valley Road, Atglen, PA 19310

Other Schiffer Books By The Author:
Ghosts in the Cemetery, 978-0-7643-2988-3, $19.99
Collecting Fluorescent Minerals, 2nd Edition, 978-0-7643-3619-5, $29.99

Other Schiffer Books on Related Subjects:
Time for Halloween Decorations, 978-0-7643-2606-6, $29.95
Timeless Halloween Collectibles, 978-0-7643-2146-3, $29.95
Halloween: Costumes and Other Treats, 978-0-7643-1410-6, $29.95

Designed by Ian Robertson
Type set in Dutch 809 BT

ISBN: 978-0-7643-3618-8
Printed in China

Schiffer Books are available at special discounts for bulk purchases for sales promotions or premiums. Special editions, including personalized covers, corporate imprints, and excerpts can be created in large quantities for special needs. For more information contact the publisher:

Published by Schiffer Publishing Ltd.
4880 Lower Valley Road
Atglen, PA 19310
Phone: (610) 593-1777; Fax: (610) 593-2002
E-mail: Info@schifferbooks.com

For the largest selection of fine reference books on this and related subjects, please visit our web site at **www.schifferbooks.com**
We are always looking for people to write books on new and related subjects. If you have an idea for a book please contact us at the above address.

This book may be purchased from the publisher.
Include $5.00 for shipping.
Please try your bookstore first.
You may write for a free catalog.

In Europe, Schiffer books are distributed by
Bushwood Books
6 Marksbury Ave.
Kew Gardens
Surrey TW9 4JF England
Phone: 44 (0) 20 8392 8585; Fax: 44 (0) 20 8392 9876
E-mail: info@bushwoodbooks.co.uk
Website: www.bushwoodbooks.co.uk

contents

acknowledgements

"No man is an island," said John Donne. This is never truer than when you are trying to put together a book. One person's knowledge is helpful, two peoples' knowledge is wonderful, but three or more are needed to be interesting and authoritative. The author wishes to thank the following people who graciously agreed to let the author photograph parts of their collections, or contributed photographs or information, and without whose help this book would not have been possible: Cindy Beebe, Georgeanne Brumbaugh, Kathy Bouchard, Lee Dunbar, Linda Dykes, Howard Edelstein, John Kleeman, William Morford, Roberta Morrison, Peter Newman, Gary & Sue Peterson, Fran Pytko, Lenny Silverman, Jenny Tarrant, James Vacca, David Warner and Timothy Zimmerman.

With a note of special thanks to Hugh A. Luck and Chris J. Russell and the Halloween Queen, Pam Apkarian-Russell, whose hospitality and depths of collection added significantly to the quality of this book.

NODDER, ca. 1915. A very scary devil's head nodder might sit on the table or a shelf at one's Halloween party.

a BRíef hístoRy of halloween

Halloween's origin was a celebration not unlike today's Thanksgiving. Unfortunately, it has been confused with early devil worship. Halloween's roots were developed in the beliefs of the Celts (pronounced "Kelts") more than 2500 years ago. The Celts were an agrarian society living mostly in northern England, Brittany, Wales, Ireland and Scotland. Little is known about the individuals of this society, except that their leaders were the Druids (sometimes called Dryads), a mysterious cult of priests and teachers. The Celts are purported to be the builders of Stonehenge, the mysterious circle of giant stones set out in a field in England.

Since the Celts were farmers and gatherers, the things that mattered to their society were the weather, the seasons and the wildlife in the areas around them. Some of Halloween's symbols evolved from this society's concerns. If the weather was too dry or too wet, they believed that forces controlling the weather were unhappy. Worship of and rituals surrounding these forces were common and repeated throughout the world in other agrarian societies. There were no established calendars at this time, only the phases of the moon and the changing of the seasons. A Celtic year ended with the harvest and the new year began with the coming of Winter.

A Druid concept was the circularity of life. There was no beginning and no end. "Death" represented not the final end of life, but several things--the end of a growing season, the harvest, Winter and the coming new year. In the spring, the leaves and trees would bloom again. This belief in the circularity of life was applied to plants, animals, and people alike.

When calendars were eventually established, the Celtic new year was set to begin on November 1 and end on October 31. The end of the year was celebrated, much as we celebrate Thanksgiving today, with harvest feasts and family get-togethers. Foods were gathered and stored for the coming Winter. Druids prayed to the god of Winter with the autumn festival of "Samhain" (pronounced "Saw-wah") also called Summer's End festival. Samhain controlled the dead or non-growing season. At these celebrations, the Druids would dress in costumes made of animal pelts, bird feathers or other natural products. It was a time to read the future, sometimes by looking into the embers of a fire, by watching the activ-

WITCH, ca. 1956. Lollipop holder made in the USA. 4 inches tall. *From the Hugh A. Luck collection.*

ity of animals, or by reading the lines in a cracked nut. Bonfires were built on hills and one clan's fire could be seen by another. The hearth fires in each home were allowed to go out and the embers of these community bonfires were then used to relight the hearth fires in a ceremony to honor the new year.

At this time of family reunion, the spirits of dead relatives were also welcomed and they too, returned home for the harvest festival. One might ask why the spirits chose this time of the year to return to their ancestral homes. Druids believed that at the end of one year and the beginning of a new year, the veil or separation between life and death, past and present was at its thinnest, allowing the spirits of their ancestors to join them for a brief time. The spirits could easily cross over to join the living.

The Celt's beliefs were simple, with good and bad spirits influencing life, death, the weather and the growth of crops. Over thousands of years, these activities solidified into annual rituals practiced in rural areas. As other societies grew up around the Celts, their local holidays were also celebrated at harvest time. An old Teutonic (German) celebration called May Eve had been celebrated as a summer holiday, but as more and more celebrants attended, the holiday was moved to October 31 since it was easier to feed more people at harvest time. The Romans celebrated an autumn festival dedicated to Pomona, goddess of the fruits and gardens. During the Romans occupation of Britain from the first to the fifth century the influences of the two cultures became intermingled. Halloween evolved from this group of festivals that conveniently took place at the end of the harvest time.

Beginning about the fifth century A.D., Christianity began spreading into the areas that the Celts occupied. The Celtic kings, at this time, were powerful overlords who controlled all aspects of Celtic life and dominated their subjects. Life was harsh. Critics and dissenters were forced into slavery or killed. In contrast to the Celtic laws, the teachings of Christ were full of compassion, forgiveness and love. Many Celts accepted and converted to this new religion. As Christians they continued their pagan festivals and saw no conflict between the Christian faith in God and competing beliefs of things magical and supernatural. The Church had no objections so long as their followers embraced the religion's principles.

Over time the Church's influence surpassed that of the Druids, but there were others vying for control of the people's spiritual life. Church leaders began to fear competition from the increasing influence of "Magic", as they called it. Magic, a religious belief in the powers of the supernatural, was winning over converts in geographical areas that the Church considered to be their own. People were abandoning the ways of the Church to practice the ways of Magic and the Church was determined to stop the loss. Among the ways that the influence of Magic was to be diminished, thought the Church, was to outlaw the heathen festivals and substitute Christian holy days in their place.

Samhain, a benign symbol of winter and the dead season, began to be portrayed as The Devil, a Christian symbol of death and evil. Devil worship became punishable by banishment or death. The Festival of Samhain was replaced about 800 A.D. by a holiday honoring the saints. November 1st was now "All Hallows Day" ("hallow" meaning "saint") and in later years November 2nd became "All Soul's Day". The evening before All Hallow's Day was All Hallow's Evening, which in its shortened form became Hallow's Even and eventually Halloween. Under the Church rule, these became days of prayer and devotion. The festival aspect was ordered abandoned for a more somber prayer day. The idea of a deeply devotional holiday caught on in some areas and was embraced in a less orthodox form in others.

The Pagan Festival Revived

In the north countries of England, Brittany and Wales, people celebrated Halloween as a deeply religious holiday. There was no trace of merriment. The day and evening was taken up with supplications to the dead. Rituals which seem bizarre by today's standards were practiced in rural areas. In some places, bones of the dead were gathered, prayed over and then returned to the crypt.

GOBLINS, ca. 1920. Tall goblin composition figure and composition candy containers in goblin shapes with a tiny cat candle holder (1.5 inches tall). German-made. 8.5 inches to 3 inches tall. *From the Hugh A. Luck collection.*

One ritual, from the 17th century, involved the "Sin Eater". Although not a Halloween ritual, it may have supplied a ghoulish flavor that attached itself to the holiday. When someone died, the sin eater was invited to the wake where he would stand over the body, eating and drinking. It was thought that his "eating the sins" of the deceased would allow that person to enter Heaven.

One can picture what visitors thought as they watched someone stuffing himself over a dead body. Tales spread and became corrupted. The image of ghouls feasting on the dead were the tales escaping from these areas. The depressing souling customs from these areas received such bad publicity that Queen Elizabeth I of England forbade all observances of All Souls Day. This helped to revive the thanksgiving-like aspect of the holiday.

the colors and images of halloween

Throughout the years that followed and although outlawed by the Church, people kept parts of their pagan rituals and beliefs. A family harvest festival was celebrated on the last day in October. It was usually held outdoors and the fall colors became the colors of Halloween - the bright oranges, yellows and browns of the harvest, the reds of the fires used to keep away the night and black for the night and leafless trees during winter. From a magical point of view, the outdoors was home to the elves, goblins, gnomes, fairies and other spirits that inhabited the woods and fields.

Fairies, the spirits of the woods, and witches, who could assume the shape of black cats, flew about on Halloween to welcome the spirits and guide them through the veil. Bonfires were lit by the holiday revellers to celebrate the harvest and by the superstitious to scare away the ghosts and witches.

Witches and Others

SCULPTURE, ca. 1985. Hand-made by Pam Bloom in England, about 8 inches tall. *From the Chris J. Russell and the Halloween Queen collection.*

The witch image is one of the most prominent during Halloween. The witch is usually portrayed as a hag-like woman with pointy chin, nose and hat, flying about on a broomstick. The word "witch" come from the word, "wica" meaning "wise one". As Druids were the religious and spiritual leaders of the Celts, wicas also held a powerful secondary position in the community. They were the doctors, fortune tellers and makers of potions and poisons. They held an important position in each community. Until the beginning of the first century, witches were rarely singled out for persecution. At that time, however, witchcraft began to be outlawed by the Roman empire on the belief that, as their influence over people was increasing, they could turn that influence against the then current leaders. From that time on, witch activities became secretive and went "underground".

A group of witches was called a coven. Witches had "conventions" several times each year, usually at the season's change, at the time of the winter equinox and summer solstice. Their gatherings at Halloween would have looked similar to the images that are so familiar in Halloween decorations. Groups of witches stirring cauldrons, others dancing, others under the influence of some hallucinogenic potion and talking in "tongues", bonfires, animal sacrifices and costumes were ever present. This was the influence of Magic that so scared the Romans and the established religion.

Superstitions grew up surrounding witches-- how to meet them and how to avoid them. One superstition held that to meet a witch, one should put their clothes on inside out and walk to a crossroads at midnight. The first person or animal met thereafter would be a witch. Warning, a black cat might be a witch in disguise.

As mentioned, organized religion did not accept competition and attempted to stamp it out or drive it out. They vilified any competing religion as being in league with the devil. The consequences were horrible for the religion not in favor. In the 13th century, during the Spanish Inquisition, thousands were killed and tortured in the name of religion. Later, this intolerance carried over to anyone not in favor. It turned against witchcraft, making witches and devil worship equal evils, hence the witch hunts in Europe from the 1400s through the 1600s and the later American Salem witch trials in the late 1600s.

During witch hunts, people were tried, tortured and killed for being in league with the devil. Witches would not be put to death until they confessed or were shown to be witches. Their bodies would be searched, looking for a mole or some secret mark of the pact with the devil. As another test they might be thrown into a body of water. If they sank and drowned, they were innocent, if they floated, that was proof of a witch. Others were pressed under huge stones. If they confessed during the torture, they were burned or hung as witches, if they died, they were considered free of the devil's control. You may say that there was no difference. They died either way. But, by not being a witch, it meant that their possessions would pass to their heirs while a witch's possessions were confiscated or burned. The unscrupulous who coveted their neighbor's wealth and lands could accuse that person of being a witch and if successful, gain their lands and knock out competition for wealth.

Have you ever thought about where the image of the devil originated? The original face of the Devil was derived from the image of a billygoat. In times when animal sacrifice was accepted, the animal of choice was a goat. A ceremonial dumping of one's sins would take place with the sins being heaped on a goat. This was the original "Scapegoat". It would be blamed for all that was wrong and then sacrificed. The goat became the personification of evil. The devil was portrayed with goat-like features--horns, pointy chin, big eyes and cloven hooves. In looking at the Halloween items in this book, notice the variations in depictions of the devil.

WALL DECORATION, ca. 1920. Die cut devil. Embossed pressed paper made in Germany. 10 inches tall.

Owls, a popular Celtic image, also became a symbol of the holiday. The owl is an animal of the night. They are more visible at harvest time, moving about silently during the night feeding on the field mice that fed on the harvest. The sounds that owls make are often eerie. They seem to be asking "Who?". Witches were said to take the shape of owls as well as cats and other animals.

The bat is another night animal that often appears in the images of Halloween. They are mysterious. They fly about silently at night and disappear during the day. They are believed to be companions of witches. With the discovery of blood sucking bats in South America, the image of the vampire as bat became embedded in popular culture. Surprisingly, during Victorian times in England, the bat was a popular image that appeared on jewelry and other decorative items.

Ghosts and spirits are one of the primary images of Halloween. During Halloween, spirits could return to their ancestral homes. The separation between the living and the dead, called the "Veil", was at its thinnest. The belief that ghosts are more common and easier to see as Halloween approaches is from the Celts. Spirits could cross the division between life and death, past and present. Even religious interpretations of the holiday consider the spirits of the dead as playing a major role in its celebration.

Ghosts left no footprints and could pass through walls without leaving a trace. They were generally invisible to the living. A Celtic method to spot ghosts was to look for them through the edges of a thin white feather. Ghosts were blamed for moving curtains in a still room, rattling chains in an attic and creating a chill of cold air across a part of one's body. Almost anything unforeseen could be explained by saying ghosts did it or were involved. Ghost "busting", which became popular with the movie of the same name in 1984, was a lucrative means of money making in olden times. Ridding homes and buildings of ghosts was a profession. It offered a service for which people would pay. To a certain extent, it is still being used in the world today. In the Chinese culture, before building a home or building, a professional spiritualist is hired to determine whether the spirits will bring luck or misfortune to the building in the future. The correct direction that the building must face is also determined. Prayers are said to placate the demons. It may seem out of reason in present times, but some people accept the spirits as real and try to appease them.

Jack-O'-Lanterns

During harvest, decorative lanterns, made out of large turnips or other fruits and vegetables, were hung outside the home. The origin of this custom of hanging lanterns arose from the custom in Scotland and Ireland of putting lanterns along the roadway to guide friends and neighbors to the harvest festival. A name given to these vegetable lanterns was "Jack of the Lantern" from a legend about a man named Jack. The story says that when Jack died, his soul could not enter Heaven because he was a miser, nor could it enter Hell because he had played jokes on the Devil. Jack's ghost was forced to wander the countryside carrying his lantern made from a turnip until Judgement day. As immigrants came to this country, the American pumpkin was substituted for the carved turnip and it became the Jack-O'-Lantern.

Jack-O'-Lantern, ca. 1920. Layered papier mache lantern with paper inserts. German-made and 6 inches tall. *From the Hugh A. Luck collection.*

Another lighted image in the night, that is rarely thought of these days, was the Will O'Wisp, an eerie glowing light that appeared over bogs and marshes. A sudden light floating over a marsh would be very frightening to the casual passerby. Scientific studies have determined that the source of these wispy lights is the combustion of gases created by the decomposition of plant matter in the swamp. Scientists seem to be able to come up with a logical reason for anything out of the ordinary. Will O'Wisps sometimes appear on early Halloween postcards.

Fortune Telling

Halloween is a night for fortune telling. In England it was called Snap-Apple or Nut-Crack Night. The name was derived from the fact that nuts and apples were abundant during the harvest. These were eaten on Halloween as symbols of the provisions saved for the winter. Additionally, they were used in fortune telling, mostly matrimonial soothsaying. Young ladies would take several nuts and name each of them after possible husbands. The nuts were thrown on burning coals and if they burned evenly, unevenly or exploded, it could be interpreted as a good match, a bad match, or spinsterhood. There were dozens of ways to determine the future and Halloween became the time to make these determinations.

Since the separation or veil between past and future was at its thinnest, it was believed that one might more easily look into the future. Early Halloween parties featured fortune telling in several forms. One, from the 18th century, was called the "Fire of Love". Half a walnut shell, containing a slip of paper with one's name, would be floated in a large tub of water. A small raft on which sticks were piled would be placed in the water and set afire. The paper in the floating nuts would catch fire and burn when they touched the raft. A few would escape burning. Those unlucky ones who did not experience the "burning passion" were destined never to marry nor find the person who would "light their fire".

Another practice involved coins and other items baked into a cake. If your piece of cake held a coin, you would be successful in business. A ring meant marriage, a thimble meant blissful life, etc.

Apples could be used in several ways to tell a person's fortune. Apple parings, would be twirled above one's head and allowed to fall to the ground behind them. The shape of the paring formed the first letter of the name of a future lover. Again, these are popular images that appear on Halloween postcards.

The Origins of Trick-or-Treating

Trick-or-Treating, going from house to house and asking for treats, has an uncertain origin. It may have started with begging. One theory says that the less fortunate could more successfully beg for food on the days of harvest celebrations. Another looks to the Christian era, where on All Souls Day, the day following Halloween, the poor would go begging from house to house for sweet cakes, called Soul-Mass Cakes, in return for their promise to say prayers for the dead. With time, the prayers and soul-mass cakes were abandoned and children came around singing for apples or candies.

Another thought was that as Halloween was a courting holiday, young people would visit their boy friend's and girl friend's homes. The suitor would bring treats for the younger children in the family and the parents would encourage the young ones to visit their neighbors, to give the couple time together, hence the idea of treats and visiting neighbors.

One other possible origin of trick-or-treating is Scotland, where, in the mid-1800s, youngsters would go out seeking treats in costume. The practice was known as "guising" (as in disguise). With the waves of immigrants coming to America after the American Civil War, Halloween became a time for guising.

Whatever the source of the idea, Halloween became a time for parties. After the turn of the century, town-sponsored costume parties, carnivals, and parades became popular. There was no concept of trick-or-treating in the United States during this period.

Trick-or-treating in the United States, seems to have begun in the northeastern part of the country, in areas populated by former immigrants from the British isles and mainland. The actual practice of trick-or-treating began from an attempt to stop the ever increasing vandalism that was occurring on Halloween.

From before the turn of the century, Halloween had been a time for "raising cain", i.e. playing tricks on neighbors. Most of these tricks were rather harmless, but over the years, the pranks became meaner. Older boys would plan a night of terrorism which could include, soaping shop windows, removing gates, changing signs, tipping over outhouses, torturing dogs and cats, removing stairs from the front of houses, and worse. They would wear disguises so that they would not be recognized. Store keepers and neighbors began giving treats (bribes) to the children to stop the tricks. This was only partially effective.

By the 1920s, the vandalism was so great that people were being hurt by the pranks and were arming themselves. In some places on Halloween groups of children were being shot at or run down by cars. Civic organizations including The Boy Scouts of America, local safety patrols, school boards, and others, took action to control the vandalism and organized supervised visiting of homes and businesses for treats and pennies. Town festivals were organized to support these supervised activities. Parents and "good" kids were on the streets to make sure that the vandals were stopped. The idea was widely accepted and was very successful.

There is no record of formal trick-or-treating before the 1920s. One early reference is in a late 1920s play by Elbridge Lyon, called "Spooks". In the play, several children in costume enter the house, dump their bags of crackers, candies, fruits, etc. onto a table and begin looking among the coins gathered for Indian Head pennies. They did not use the term, "trick-or-treating" and the play does not further explain where they obtained their treats.

By the 1930s, the custom was established and was spreading across the country. The expression "trick-or-treat" became the Halloween greeting during the late 1930s or early 1940s. In many places the expression was slightly different. An example is "trick for a treat", meaning I will do a trick for you, such as sing a song or tell a joke, if you give me a treat. There are many regional variations.

In 1950, the United Nations became involved in the American Halloween celebration and created UNICEF. The initials stand for United Nations International Children's Emergency Fund. The fund was set up to help sick and hungry children all over the world. Trick-or-treaters were given orange containers to collect pennies and nickels as they went from house to house. Trick-or-treaters these days rarely carry the orange container for UNICEF although it is still in existence.

NEW YORKER, 1945. Magazine cover.

The Sinister Side

Despite all good intentions, Halloween has a dark side. It plays very little part in today's celebration but less than lovely people took advantage of the holiday's customs for their own purposes. Devil worship and satanic rituals seem to make the news each year around Halloween and stories of apples and candy with sharp objects inside always appear after the holiday. Hard and fast rules given to children before trick or treating include, travel in groups and do not eat anything until it is brought home and parents have inspected it.

In the two and a half decades following the turn of the century, Halloween was noted to be a time when young hooligans went out and did damage to property in the name of "just having a little fun". This "fun" was usually had on Halloween night. When the holiday was changed, with the introduction of trick-or-treating, the night before Halloween became the time for errant youth to roam the streets and alleys looking for trouble. The night before Halloween has different names in different areas. Depending on location it is called Cabbage Night, Mischief Night, Prank Night, Gate Night, and the dreaded Devil's Night.

POSTCARD, ca. 1911. Halloween postcards show the superstition, party activities and spirits of the holiday. One of the interesting categories is the pranks of Halloween. This one shows kids changing shop signs.

Most pranks have been substantially reduced to soaping windows, putting shaving cream on cars, throwing toilet paper over trees, throwing eggs at cars or neighbors' houses, smashing pumpkins, and bopping others on the head with socks filled with flour. There is a small, deviant population who set fires on this night. In the suburbs and rural areas, fire departments are always on call to put out burning piles of leaves. In some urban areas, the dreaded Devil's Night has arsonists setting vacant buildings afire. Unfortunately, this night of trouble reflects badly on Halloween. There are calls for curfews and an end to Halloween itself.

UNKNOWN, ca. 1911. Kids doing Halloween pranks and games. *From the Hugh A. Luck collection.*

Being a holiday of disguises, Halloween unfortunately has historically been a time of attacks on minorities by disguised persons. The most infamous event in recent history is the German "Krystalnacht" or night of broken glass. In the 1930s, a new German leader, Adolf Hitler, was ascending to power. The Jews of Germany, some who controlled the largest banks and many who were local merchants, were targeted by Hitler's paramilitary force, the Brown Shirts, to be beaten, intimidated and driven from the country. On Halloween, thousands of Brown Shirts put on masks and roamed the streets breaking the windows in stores, setting afire Jewish owned businesses and beating and killing any Jews that could be found. The Nazi press played it up as just some youthful vandals on Halloween. It was the beginning of the rise of Hitler and many religious Jews still shun Halloween several generations later. Hopefully, Halloween is moving towards harmless fun rather than demented and hurtful acts.

MAGAZINE, 1940. *Child Life* has artwork by wonderful
illustrators. These display well and can make a great inexpensive collection.

halloween in america

The Scottish may be credited with bringing Halloween to the United States. During the period after the American Civil War, the United States saw an incredible influx of immigrants. The earliest symbols of Halloween which appear at the turn of the century, include Scottish thistles, tartan designs and other traditional Scottish themes indicating its Scottish origins. It is often thought to be an Irish holiday, but the earliest decorations never show shamrocks, leprechauns, etc.

Halloween has become an American holiday. Although its celebration is harmless, it continues to come under fire from religious groups. Many believe it is a form of devil worship or alternatively a devout religious holiday. In practice, today's Halloween celebrations rarely put emphasis on the doings of the devil or worship of the dark side, nor are they particularly religious. Halloween's images are designed to be scary but not life threatening. These images have, over the years of its celebration in America, remained somewhat constant. When the activities are aimed at children, the ghosts, black cats and Jack-O'-Lanterns are usually smiling and rather tame. The images aimed at young adults are more frightening - scary witches, flaming skulls and snarling ghouls - because they demand it. Since the turn of the century, Halloween's scary images have been portrayed in decorations made specifically for parties.

A holiday associated with Halloween occurs in Mexico. All Souls day is celebrated as Dia de los Muertos - the Day of the Dead. It honors the dead with celebrations, feasts, parades, fireworks, and prayer. Food, such as pan de muerto, a bread that looks like twisted bones and candies, spun sugar skulls with candy crowns, are made and sold in bakeries and food stores. Store windows, homes, and public places are decorated with images of skeletons - skeletons on bicycles, skeletons doing every day chores and even animal skeletons. The celebration is carried to the cemetery where parties are held at graveside to honor the dead. Some families keep the bones of their relatives in tombs and bring them out for the celebration. The United States Latino communities are slowly embracing the holiday and bringing some of its imagery up north.

Halloween parties in the United States became popular in Victorian times. Parties during the 1880s and 1890s were held to bring young people together. The decorations were natural seasonal products such as pumpkins, vegetables, corn stalks, etc. By 1910, several American manufacturers were making or importing party products specifically for Halloween, such as pressed paper Jack-O'-Lanterns, rattles, vegetable people figurines and paper decorations.

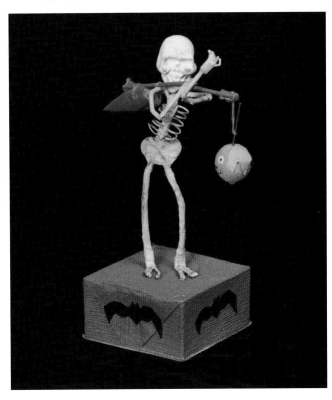

CANDY CONTAINER, ca. 1920. A fabulous image of a traveling skeleton with vegetables on a pole on a crepe-covered box, composition over wire, made in Germany. 6.5 inches tall. *From the Chris J. Russell and the Halloween Queen collection.*

Many of the earliest decorations were made in Germany. Imports from Germany stopped during World War I (probably from 1916-1919) and American companies took over to fill the demand. Dating the early products is approximate, since some products were unchanged for a number of years. One early American company that produced Halloween supplies was the Dennison Paper Company. Their output of Halloween decorations was incredible and the quality of their product was excellent, from the designs used to the execution of the item on paper. Since Halloween decorations were usually thrown out after the holiday rather than saved like Christmas decorations, the pieces available to collectors are rare.

An invaluable source of information about what was available and when it was produced are the Dennison's *Bogie Books* and later their *Party Magazine*, which replaced the *Bogie Book* in 1927. *Bogie Books* showed the products available and how to decorate with them. They also offered Halloween stories and recipes. After a first issue in 1909, they officially began issuing the booklet in 1912 (the 1924 edition is marked "12th edition") and continued yearly. The 1912 *Bogie Book* starts as follows:

BOGIE BOOK, 1917. By Dennison.

Welcome. Wherein are collated ideas for the Hallowe'en hostess which we believe will be instrumental in making a jolly and characteristic Witch Night Party. Two points have been kept in mind throughout - to give practical suggestions that can be carried out easily with little labor and expense and to offer fresh material that will be unusual as well as appropriate.

The date for this old-time celebration is always October 31st; the crucial moment, 12 o'clock. To be sure, the original observance of All Hallowed Eve has become somewhat distorted through the years, but the fun it affords young people in its present manner of keeping cannot be gainsaid and needs no changing.

Hallowe'en is the night when a magic spell enthralls the earth. Witches rule. Bogies, Brownies, Elves and Dryads use their power and all things creeping have no fear. Superstition proves true, witchery asserts itself, and the future may be read in a thousand ways. No occasion gives more chance for enjoyment, no party is more gay than the one this night.

Each *Bogie Book* contained 24 to 32 pages of decorations, party ideas, stories, room decorating, recipes and costumes. The costumes capture the essence of then current fashions, while the articles and language show the spirit of rural America.

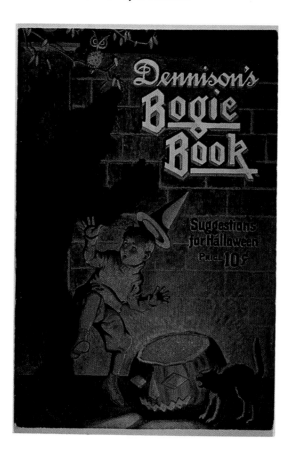

BOGIE BOOK, 1923. By Dennison.

collections

A collection of Halloween items need not be old nor large. Many new collectors and most experienced collectors will drool over some of the pieces in this book. Some collectors have been searching for Halloween items for over 20 years. When they started, people used to ask why they would collect such junk. Time has proved them to be visionaries. Will you be a visionary and pick up things today that will be valuable and sought after in the future?

Let this book be your incentive to add current items to your collection. Wonderful items are being made today that will be difficult to find in the future. Check out Ghostbusters, The Nightmare Before Christmas and other recent movie items. They are clearly adaptable for Halloween. Many non-Halloween items can be used for Halloween. Unusual pieces such as ugly candlesticks, a witch weather vane, skull drinking mugs, a plastic rat and other thought provoking pieces make good Halloween decorations that add flavor and ambience to any Halloween party.

A source for older decorations may be stationary and general stores in early October. See if they have any old Halloween items in their basements. Visit antique paper and advertising shows and ask your favorite antique dealer to keep an eye out (or even pull an eye out) for anything Halloween.

Valuing Halloween Memorabilia

Valuing Halloween memorabilia is difficult in this quickly changing field. One can use a "Supply and Demand" valuation or what would a willing buyer and a willing seller agree to as a value? An examination of the components of value are helpful. A valuable item is usually rare, but a rare item is not always valuable. A rare paper piece, of which only one or two are known may not have the broad appeal of a Halloween candy container of which there are 20 known. The rarity factor is not the main determinant of value.

Take the example of a collector who is attempting to find a certain item for his collection. He values that item many times higher than another person who already has one. That collector might be willing to pay $1000 for one piece, but would he buy a second or a third at the same price? It depends upon who is buying, the availability and how badly he wants the item. Due to increased competition, collectors on the East coast and the West coast of the United States often pay more than those in the central portions of the country.

Things to consider when collecting Halloween items:

Condition: Condition is an important criteria. An item in mint condition may be worth several times more than one in very fine condition. Damage to a visible part may be a major problem. An item with a piece missing may be worth 25% of one with the piece present. Repair is often possible, but to repair the item, one needs parts or another of the same with that part. Ask yourself if the price is still a bargain when you have to locate and cannibalize another piece for parts. The items in this book are priced in excellent condition although the actual piece shown may vary from good to mint in the box.

Original Parts: Pieces should have original parts and finishes. Refinishing an item will in most instances, not increase its value and will often decrease its value. An "honest" finish or patina, indicating that the item has seen use, is preferred.

Availability or "Will I ever find another?": Some items are always available at antique shows or specialized dealers. A good example, at this time, are the papier mache lanterns from the 1950s. Ask yourself if it is just a matter of dollars to acquire an example or is this a once in a lifetime chance to find that item? With a once-in-a-lifetime item, condition should not be the major determining factor. Many items were ephemeral or short lived. All that is left may just be a relic or remembrance of the whole item. On those items, you may never get another chance to buy one and the person behind you may be waiting for you to put it down so that he or she can buy it.

Demand: What does it mean to you? To those growing up in the period covered by this book, some items bring back a flood of memories. To some people, seeing an item is enough. To others, possessing it is required, regardless of the price. There are collectors aplenty in the field of Halloween collecting and the asking price reflects this enormous demand.

Buy the Best: In comparing Halloween collectibles to other collecting fields, it is expected that prices on Halloween items will continue to rise. Higher prices may be a blessing in disguise. Some people have no incentive to sell a piece for only a few dollars, but if they can get "a lot of money" they will sell a piece. You will pay more but you will get a piece that you may never have another chance to own. Collections can be put together for very little money, but, as has been proven true in every field of antique collecting, the best pieces in the best condition have held or increased in value at a greater rate than the more common pieces. Buy the best that you can afford. Remember, you will rarely regret having paid too much for an item, but you will always regret the good pieces that got away.

Cost: A Halloween collection need not cost a great deal of money. Some people collect new items. Joining an organization or subscribing to a magazine can provide hundreds of leads to current Halloween items. Using your imagination, a nice collection can be put together within your budget. Exhibiting your collection at a local library can generate new leads to the type of material that you collect.

Investment: I discourage people from "investing" in collectibles. Collecting should be for fun and not just profit. Profits will be come if you collect the items that you enjoy and at some later time decide to sell. Buying for investment only, means never playing with your things. They could get scratched or broken. Buying, selling and trading items can help you hone a collection to those items that bring you the most pleasure.

Locating items: Halloween items can be found at garage sales, antique stores, antique toy shows, flea markets, mail auctions and through ads in the antique collector newspapers. A good start may be to run an ad in your local newspaper or do an exhibit of your collection at a local library. Both of these should provide you with numerous leads. Try to meet other collectors, they can provide leads to sources that you have not considered and they provide potential trading partners.

It is often said that a price guide is out of date the moment that it is published. Do not let that affect your use of a value guide. A value guide is comparative. It allows you to compare two items to determine if they are of comparable value. It is useful in buying and trading and it can help give you a feel for the rarity of a piece.

Remember, two is a coincidence, three is a collection. Happy hunting!

Invitations

Halloween was the perfect time for a party and no party could be announced without an invitation. The Halloween party invitation was often a small work of art. In 1912, Dennison suggested ways to make your own invitations in the shape of cats or bats or puzzle invitations. One, a puzzle invitation, was prepared, then torn into pieces and sent for one's friends to reassemble. Terminology suggested for the invitations is quaint by today's standards.

> When Leaf is Red
> And Night is dark,
> Come masqueraded
> For a lark

or

> If you'd learn your fate
> or your destined mate,
> Accept this invitation.
> Have no dread or fear,
> On that fateful night, mortals seldom sight
> The revels I can show you
> And the antics queer.

INVITATIONS, ca. 1919. Two postcard invitations for Halloween. *From the Chris J. Russell and the Halloween Queen collection.*

By 1915, Dennison and others were selling pre-printed invitations. They are often masterpieces of artwork. The imagery is wonderful with witches and ghouls inviting you to join the party given by the hosts. The artwork is very much in the then current style, such as art nouveau, mission, or art deco. Invitations were available as today, in packs of 8 or so and also available as postcards.

The present value of these early invitations gives little hint to their rarity. They make a nice display when framed together as a group. Quality varies dramatically. Some early invitations contain seven or eight colors and are extremely detailed. Others are two to three colors and use a more cartoonish style of illustration. This is not to demean cartoon styles, since known cartoon characters, such as Mickey Mouse or Felix the Cat, on Halloween invitations are rare.

Crepe Paper

CREPE PAPER, ca. 1916. Witches on Pumpkins. 20 inches wide by 10 feet long. Made by Dennison #858

Crepe paper rolls were among the earliest Halloween decorations and one of the most flexible to utilize. Crepe was used to decorate walls, table and even made into costumes. It could be formed into ropes, Spanish moss, ruffles, or fringe. The design appears to be silk screened onto the paper and can be found with 4 to 6 colors in one design, although 3 colors seems to be the standard. In 1912 Dennison made 4 Halloween designs in wide decorated crepe - "Witch and Kettle" on an orange background (catalog #948), "Witch Parade" also on orange (#985), "Cats and Bats" available on white or orange (#986, #987) and "Yellow Pumpkins" on black (#988). These rolls were 20 inches wide, 10 feet long and cost ten cents. Other crepe products were napkins, table covers, streamers and doilies. By 1916, there were 7 designs in wide decorated crepe, 6 of them new - "Cloud Effect With Witches" (#825), "Pumpkin Men And Cats" (#827), "Jack-O'-Lantern And Ghosts" (#828), "Dancing Witches" (#829), "Bogies In Wood" (#82), "Black Witch" (#83), "Ghosts And Witches Tug Of War" (#84) and "Yellow Pumpkins" on black (#988). The cost per roll was fifteen cents.

By 1921, the cost was thirty cents and additional designs were "Cats On Orange" (#833), "Flying Witch on Orange" (#834), "Witch And Cobweb on Orange" (#835), "Halloween Roof Scene" (#836), "Halloween Ground Scene" (#837), "Owl And Moon" (#838), "Gobolink" (#839) and the old standard by this time "Yellow Pumpkins" on black (#988) which continued to be available up until the 1930s. New designs were added every year.

Dennison was not the only maker of decorated crepe. Others makers of memorable designs were Bainbridge and American Tissue Mills. The crepe imagery is wonderful and as the pattern is repeated, one matted 18 inch panel is often sold as a complete decorative item. One very unusual piece, circa 1915, showed witches flying on Wright Brothers-style airplanes. Airplanes were just getting off the ground in the 1910s. The use of the 20 inch wide crepe seems to have slowly vanished after the 1930s, only to reappear after the war. Pieces from the 1950s were printed in two colors and available in 5 or 6 foot lengths. Had the crepe format continued to present times, one would expect to see a pattern called "Witches in Space Shuttle". Old crepe may be flammable, so if you use it in decorating for Halloween, keep it away from any open flames.

Costumes

Of the things most closely associated with Halloween, one immediately thinks of costumes. From the time that Druids dressed up in feathers or furs, costumes have played an important part in the holiday. Today, grown-ups wearing Halloween costumes are stared at but accepted in banks, supermarkets and other retail businesses. Provided of course, that it is Halloween.

The Halloween costume grew popular in America during the 1880s and 1890s. Dressing in costume to go to a Halloween party was fun and became acceptable. The early costumes were home made. Women's magazines gave instructions for making them. The earliest *Bogie Books* gave tips for making costumes out of crepe paper. Dennison and others began selling paper costumes in the 1910s. One interesting costume item offered, was the Dennison's crepe paper apron trimmed in cloth. Not many have survived. Dennison also made paper costumes. They were meant to be worn once and discarded. Very few of them have survived either and although rarer than most other Halloween pieces, generally do not command much money.

COSTUME, ca. 1958. A Ben Cooper Disney Tinkerbell costume with a thin plastic one piece mask.

Sears Roebuck and Company offered their first pre-made Halloween costumes about 1930. By the 1940s, many companies such as Collegeville, Ben Cooper and Halco were making tens of thousands of ready to wear Halloween costumes. The cost was regularly under $3.00 per costume with mask. Usually the material was a thin fabric with the design silkscreened onto it. Prices of old costumes are not high and they make a very displayable collection.

Costumes reflect the popular themes of the time they were made. The character costumes of the late 1940s and early 1950s are collected by comic and other character collectors as well as Halloween collectors. Disney characters were popular and many that appeared in 1940s and 1950s movies were sold as costumes in the 1950s. Pirates, skeletons, and witches were also popular in the 1950s. Spacemen were seen

in the years 1962 and 1969. Hobos have been popular from the 1950s to recent times. In the 1960s, television characters were popular. In recent years, numerous trick or treaters were spotted wearing Darth Vader, Ninja Turtles, Freddie Kruger, and more recently Batman, Barney and Alladin.

In the 1970s, the costume bodies were being made of vinyl and the legs of cloth. By the end of the 1970s, most inexpensive costumes were all vinyl. They finally degenerated to being nothing more than vinyl smocks with a mask. It is only recently, with the increasing sale of Halloween goods, that the high quality silk screened cloth costumes have made their return. Of course the prices are now $20.00 to $40.00 or more.

Hats and Masks

The origin of party hats may stem from Celtic times. Parties were celebrated with party hats and wonderful Halloween hats can be found. These may have been the perfect thing for those who refused to wear a costume all evening long. As with most Halloween items, the hats were rarely saved. Dennison began offering one style of crepe paper hats in 1916 at 5 cents each. In 1921 they had four styles of hats and began offering paper masks at 15 cents each. Many of these crepe paper hats were quite complex, being assembled with sewn seams and applied decorations.

PARTY HATS, 1912. From the Dennison *Bogie Book*.

There were some great Halloween party hats that were lithographed in many colors with wonderful images. Hats were also made in tiny sizes so that little girls could have their own Halloween party for their dolls and teddy bears. Alternatively, perhaps these little hats were made for elves and fairies to wear on Halloween. Hats and masks can be found with simple designs to multicolored intricate designs and images. One form of mask was a cheese cloth material that was sized, formed and often painted. Many hats and masks were printed in Germany, Japan, or the United States. Prices are usually reasonable.

Plates

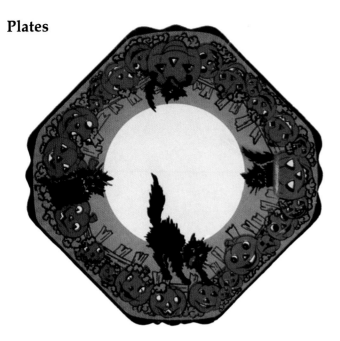

PARTY PLATE, ca. 1930. C.A. Reed Co. of Williamsport, Pennsylvania was one of the major plate and napkin producers.

Halloween paper plates from before 1950 are difficult to find but may not be especially valuable at this time. Many collectors have not yet discovered their charm. The quality of the illustrations on some plates makes them a good decorative item in any Halloween collection. They were among the most expendable items, so for the person looking to keep their collection small, you will not find too many plates. As Halloween collectors get together in the future, paper plate trading may be a great way to expand a collection. A good source of older plates may be your local general store or any store that used to sell party supplies. They may have old stock in their basement or on a back shelf that has sat there for 20 or more years. It can often be bought at a discount from the low price listed on the package.

Trick or Treat Bags

The earliest trick or treat bags, used to gather goodies from neighbors, were probably plain cloth sacks or small baskets. The paper or cloth bag decorated with Halloween scenes probably did not make its first appearance until the late 1930s. During the war years - 1941 to 1945 - few commercial bags were made, but by the 1950s, numerous stores and companies were offering bags with their names or products shown. In the 1960s, larger decorated shopping bags were popular. Most stores stopped offering nice bags by the 1970s and in the 1980s, the Halloween designed bags began to be sold rather than given away. Some stores offered their regular shopping bags

with the addition of a Halloween design and warnings about safety on Halloween. The bags were often thrown out or ripped apart by the young trick or treaters so they are actually very hard to find.

TRICK OR TREAT BAG, ca. 1964. Distributed by Esso 14 inches tall, not including handle.

Noisemakers

ROLLING HORNS, ca. 1955. Hard plastic whistles in Halloween colors made in the USA. Some wheels replaced. 5 inches tall. *From the Hugh A. Luck collection.*

One of the most common items for Halloween was the noisemaker. Noisemakers came in many styles. There were whistles, horns, rattles, tambourines, clickers, bells, tin can rattles, ratchet styles and others, such as the tin frying pan noisemakers. The earliest type was probably the ratchet style. This was a wooden design that was used hundreds if not thousands of years ago. The Halloween versions are usually multilayered ratchets with the addition of a Halloween figure or head attached. For the collector, these bear close review since a simple $10 ratchet can be sold for much more with the addition of a Halloween part of a figure. After the ratchet style, the paper tambourines and horns seem to have appeared. Following the introduction of the tambourines were the tin noisemakers - rattles and horns. There are many exceptions to these rules and plenty of overlap with many styles being made at the time others were being made. The graphics or style can give you a clue as to the age of the piece and they make a very displayable collection.

Candy Containers

Some of the earliest candy containers were glass figural bottles or composition material in the shape of a vegetable or cornucopia. These evolved into vegetable people, witches, cats, pumpkin men and other scary little creatures. Candy containers are among the most difficult to find Halloween items that collectors seek. The variety is great and the creations are often incredibly detailed. The addition of glass eyes, noses, or some mechanical aspect adds a premium to the pieces. With the great variety, there are candy containers to suit every budget, but even the more recent ones seem to be offered at premium prices.

Dating these early containers is guesswork combined with knowledge gleaned from catalogs. Some designs may have been made for several years, while others may have been made for only one season. Candy sellers probably did not throw out pieces that did not sell. Instead, they put them away for another year until they were eventually sold. Most candy containers were filled with what we would call candy pills.

The earliest character or figural containers were made of glass and have been collected by glass candy container collectors for many years. About 1912, the Germans started making containers of "composition". Composition is a plaster-like material with the addition of glue, wood pulp, hair or paper fiber to give it a lighter feel and greater strength than simple plaster.

At the same time composition pieces were being made, other containers and lanterns were being made of paperboard pulp that was formed in a mold, pressed and heated to make convex surfaces. Some early pressed paperboard was then coated with composition and painted. Pressed paperboard was made in the teens, 1920s and probably as late as 1950s.

There was a great deal of overlap of the different production methods so exact dating of the composition and formed, pressed paperboard candy containers is difficult. For the most part, both were made in Germany. Since United States trade with Germany was affected by World War I, imports appear to have stopped sometime in 1916 and picked up again by 1920. Most composition containers are believed to have been sold circa 1920 but they may date from as early as 1912 or as late as 1930.

Many Dennison crepe paper-covered candy containers were homemade in the teens and 1920s. Variation and variety are often very creative. In the 1920s, Japan began to manufacture molded cardboard and papier mache variations, often imitating the German styles of several years before. As time progressed, the Japanese style evolved and some of the items are masterpieces in miniature.

Over the past 20 years, as the German containers became too expensive, collectors began to pick up the Japanese versions. As these too, became difficult to find, collectors have moved on to the hard plastic models. The use of hard plastic started in the 1950s. Most seem to have been made or sold by Rosen Company of Rhode Island which appears to still be in business. This 1950s plastic is sometimes mistakenly called "celluloid". Real celluloid was originally produced in the 1880s with a clear version being found on old political pins. There are examples of very thin colored celluloid made in Halloween rattles and figures during the 1920s and through the 1930s. Real celluloid is very fragile and flammable and a piece in good condition can be a prized item in any collection.

FIGURE, ca. 1928. Pumpkin man articulated figure, composition, made in Germany. 4.75 inches tall in sitting position. *From the Chris J. Russell and the Halloween Queen collection.*

Jack-O'-Lanterns

The symbol that most captures the Halloween spirit is the Jack-O'-Lantern or carved pumpkin. The earliest Jack-O'-Lanterns are made of composition or pressed paper. Composition resembles plaster of Paris. They had cutouts for the eyes, nose, and mouth which were often backed with thin colored paper. When a candle was put inside, the Jack- O'-Lantern grinned. By the 1920s, pressed and formed paperboard and die cut flat paperboard were beginning to supersede composition. This was followed by papier mache in the 1930s. A lighter papier mache resembling egg carton material came into use in the late 1930s and thereafter. Lithographed flat cardboard lanterns also began to appear in the 1930s. Plastic entered the scene in the 1950s and the candle was replaced by the battery and bulb. Rather than go into great detail about the construction, look at the illustrations to get an idea of age and style.

LANTERN, ca. 1920. A pressed and formed paperboard Jack-O'-Lantern with tissue paper inserts. 5 inches tall, most likely made in Germany.

The term Jack-O'-Lantern may be applied to any Halloween lantern regardless of its shape, color or figure, but the standard Jack-O'-Lantern is a "carved" face on a pumpkin. There are Jack-O'-Lanterns, in the style of the 1920s, that are made of painted pressed paperboard and marked "West Germany" that have appeared on the market recently. West Germany did not exist until after the end of the Second World War. Many are in mint condition and priced reasonably while others are being offered at top dollar and sold as being very old. They are a great addition to a collection when the price is not out of line.

Inside Decorations

CUT OUTS, ca. 1920s Made by Dennison. *From the Chris J. Russell and the Halloween Queen collection.*

Decorating the home for Halloween parties was part of the fun of a Halloween party. While most people decorated modestly, Halloween lent itself to extraordinary decorating. As a popular current Halloween party book states, there is no way to over-decorate for your Halloween party. More is better. Most of the early decoration was paper. The earliest was embossed and die cut cardboard or pressed paper board. As much of the printing industry was in Germany, many of the earlier pieces were made there. When the first World War started, dealers looked for sources other than Germany. One of the early quality makers was the Beistle Company. They produced hundreds of designs starting in the 1920s. Most were printed in 3 or more colors.

In the 1920s, honey comb tissue was added to many pieces to give a three dimensional effect. The honey comb tissue had been used as early as the 1880s on valentines and has lasted into present times. The honeycomb material was a thin tissue that can be very fragile. Good repairs to damaged pieces can be made with white glue and some patience.

The demand for paper party goods was growing tremendously until the 1929 start of the great depression. During the depression, demand continued but not as robustly. People never stopped partying as it was inexpensive and fun. The War years of the 1940s curtailed the public's spirit to have adult Halloween parties. Children's parties remained although party supplies dried up and became less available. Few American companies were in a position to make the product due to war material shortages. Halloween took a backseat until the end of the War, when the baby boom began in the 1950s. The 1950s ushered in a new era of Halloween parties for children and a new crop of decorations. This boom lasted until the mid-1960s and then slowed down through the 1970s. It began to return in the mid-1980s and has been climbing to present.

The volume and variety of goods made during the boom years is staggering. This book can show but a representative sample of the items produced. The fact that an item does not appear in the book is not indicative of its rarity or value. Some very rare items were unavailable to be photographed and other common material was left out to make way for the nicer material. Additionally many pieces were made in series and often the intent was to show a representative sample rather than the entire series.

Postcards

Postcards are the most popular Halloween collectible. There were thousands made and they range from the simple cards with "Happy Halloween" and a picture of a cat, to the elaborate cards with numerous colors, embossing, and gilding. Picture postcards began appearing in late 1800s and by the early 1900s, millions were being produced every year. 1910 is considered to be the height of the golden age of postcards. Halloween cards can be found from the first years of the 1900s to present. Many were commissioned from the leading artists of the day. Notable artist names are Clapsaddle, Schmucker, Brundage, Frexis, Gibbs, and others. Notable publisher names are Winsch, Wolf, Gibson, and Tuck.

Prices for these cards in mint condition can be astounding, but a wonderful Halloween postcard collection can be assembled very reasonably if you will accept cards showing some wear or lacking the name of a known artist. Since the variety is vast, it can be overwhelming to collect every type. Many collectors look for a single topic. Topics for collecting include vegetable characters, children being frightened or playing games, witches, Halloween pranks, fortune telling, legends, superstitions, black cats, and bats.

WOLF, ca. 1910. Two postcards published by Wolf Publishing. *From the Hugh A. Luck collection.*

Again, Germany was the center of the world's printing until the first World War. Portland, Maine became the American capital of postcard printing during the war when the imports were stopped. The quality is often less than that found on German-made cards, but some incredibly nice cards were produced in America.

Outside Decoration

There are few outside decorations for Halloween that were commercially made before 1960. Examples exist of weathervanes made by talented craftsmen and boot scrapers made in the shape of a witch. The interesting decorations are those done by individuals for their homes or businesses. The idea of decorating the outside of one's home was usually kept simple up to the 1960s. A few cornstalks, Jack-O'-Lanterns and perhaps a scarecrow were considered to be "going all out".

The most decorated place in a community was usually the local farm stand. As a form of advertising, the stand might create a graveyard with Jack-O'-Lanterns, ghosts, and scarecrow people. People came and bought their produce and the children were amused.

Over the past 20 years, the idea of creating a scary setting for Halloween has grown. Now, simple to unbelievably complex displays appear in many neighborhoods. The idea is to create the atmosphere of a haunted house or small country graveyard that will both frighten and amuse the neighbors or party guests. The talent that can be displayed varies. Usually a child is in charge of the decorations, but when the skills of a creative friend or parent are added, the results can be impressive.

New commercial products for the outdoors appear every season. Styrofoam gravestones, large glowing skeletons, plastic rats, plastic trash bags with Jack-O'-Lantern or ghoul faces to hold the fallen and raked leaves can be found in most communities. The best displays are usually homemade. Plastic rarely seems to capture the seasonal atmosphere as well as natural products but over time, the products keep improving.

In the 1990s a new decorating idea has becoming popular - the seasonal flag. Hundreds of flags are beginning to appear during autumn, showing pumpkins and leaves, ghosts or Halloween scenes. When the season is through, one puts that flag away and rolls out the next one with Santas or snowmen.

Bakelite jewelry sometimes incorporated scarecrows and black cats in the art deco style. Jack-O'-Lanterns and other Halloween specific designs rarely appear until the 1950s. They then appeared in plastic pins. Many 1950s plastic pins had "googly eyes". There has been a resurgence of Halloween pins and jewelry in the 1980s.

Magazine covers make a striking display or a nice "portfolio" collection. Look at the section showing *New Yorker* covers and children's magazine covers. Generally the covers are more interesting than the articles inside of children's magazines, although the articles from the 1930s should show the beginnings of Trick or Treating. The *New Yorker*, prior to the early 1940s, did not produce a special cover for the Halloween issue. Their current covers for Halloween are often political or current event related. There are numerous other magazines amd magazine advertisements that give a flavor for the past Halloweens.

VICTORIAN HOUSE. This home is decorated to give a very "Adams Family" feeling. There is a nice graveyard in the front and the porch is covered with spider webs, bats and skeletons and ghouls frolic on the roof.

Miscellaneous

Miscellaneous items include jewelry, games, candle holders, and other figural items with a Halloween theme. Often these items were not made for Halloween but were adopted for the Holiday. In jewelry, during Victorian times, spiders, bats and owl pins in precious metals were popular in England and on the continent. Through the 1910s, pins in Halloween shapes were made in Germany. 1920s and 1930s

NEW YORKER, 1989. Magazine cover.

invitations

INVITATION, ca. 1915. This Invitation was included in the Peggy's Halloween Party Box. *From the Chris J. Russell and the Halloween Queen collection.*

INVITATIONS, ca. 1896. 2 postcard invitations for Halloween that seem to be later than the date of the party - Oct. 28, 1896. Published by Gibson Art. *From the Chris J. Russell and the Halloween Queen collection.*

INVITATION, ca. 1920. Made by Dennison. *From the Chris J. Russell and the Halloween Queen collection.*

INVITATIONS, ca. 1915. Four postcard invitations for Halloween. *From the Chris J. Russell and the Halloween Queen collection.*

INVITATIONS, ca. 1919 Six postcard invitations for Halloween. *From the Chris J. Russell and the Halloween Queen collection.*

INVITATION, ca. 1920. Made in USA, maker unknown.

INVITATIONS, ca. 1920. Made in USA.

INVITATION, ca. 1920. Multipurpose invitation that could announce a ball, a party, a dinner or a card party. Made in USA.

INVITATION, ca. 1934. A great "mechanical" invitation made by Beistle. *From the Chris J. Russell and the Halloween Queen collection.*

Invitation ca 1930, made in U.S.A.

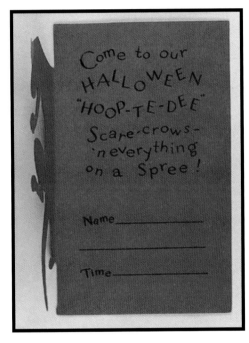

INVITATION, ca. 1930. Pumpkin-shaped, Made by Gibson in the USA.

INVITATION, ca. 1940. Made in USA by the Buzza Co. of Minneapolis.

SQUEEKERS, ca. 1915. Lithographed cardboard accordion squeekers. German-made. 2.75 inches tall. *From the Chris J. Russell and the Halloween Queen collection.*

INVITATION, ca. 1945. Made in USA.

HORN, ca. 1916. "Acorn Squash Head". Made in Germany, composition over pressed paperboard. 7 inches high. This is an exceptional noisemaker. It is big, complex and has great character. *From the Chris J. Russell and the Halloween Queen collection.*

HORN, ca. 1920. "Eggplant Head". Made in Germany, pressed paperboard. 4 inches high. *From the Chris J. Russell and the Halloween Queen collection.*

JACK-O'-LANTERN RATTLES, ca. 1915 and 1950 (with crepe frill). These small noisemaker drums on a stick were filled with pebbles or rice. They are very fragile and one with both drums intact is a great find. The drumhead is about 4 inches in diameter.

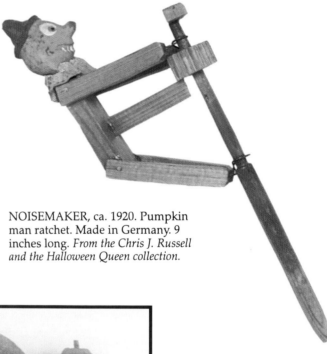

NOISEMAKER, ca. 1920. Pumpkin man ratchet. Made in Germany. 9 inches long. *From the Chris J. Russell and the Halloween Queen collection.*

NOISEMAKERS, ca. 1920. Tambourine horn with a cat design and Jack-O'-Lantern ratchet. Both made in Germany. Horn is 8 inches long. *From the Chris J. Russell and the Halloween Queen collection.*

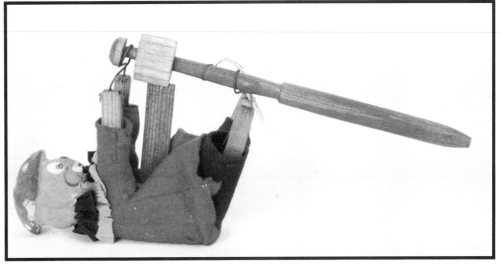

NOISEMAKER, ca. 1920. Pumpkin man ratchet. Made in Germany. 9 inches long. *From the Chris J. Russell and the Halloween Queen collection.*

NOISEMAKER, ca. 1920. Black cat ratchet. Made in Germany. 9 inches long. *From the Chris J. Russell and the Halloween Queen collection.*

NOISEMAKER, ca. 1920. Jack-O'-Lantern man on black cat ratchet. Made in Germany. 12 inches long. *From the Chris J. Russell and the Halloween Queen collection.*

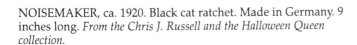

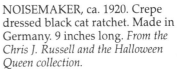

NOISEMAKER, ca. 1920. Crepe dressed black cat ratchet. Made in Germany. 9 inches long. *From the Chris J. Russell and the Halloween Queen collection.*

HORN, ca. 1920. Pumpkin figures made in Germany, pressed paperboard. 5.5 inches and 4.25 inches high. *From the Chris J. Russell and the Halloween Queen collection.*

NOISEMAKER, ca. 1925. A lithographed tin rattle with Halloween designs and wooden handle. 4.5 inches across.

NOISEMAKER, ca. 1925. Wooden banjo to create a Halloween racket. Kid size, made in USA. *From the Chris J. Russell and the Halloween Queen collection.*

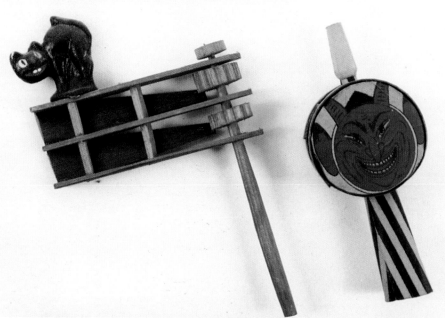

NOISEMAKERS, ca. 1920. Black cat ratchet and tambourine horn with a devil design. Both made in Germany. Horn is 6 inches long. *From the Chris J. Russell and the Halloween Queen collection.*

HORN, ca. 1925. Pumpkin figure made in Germany, pressed paperboard. 4.5 inches high. *From the Chris J. Russell and the Halloween Queen collection.*

SAXOPHONES, ca. 1925. Lithographed paper over pressed cardboard. These are 8 inches tall and the complete set would have had one more horn with a skull head bowl. The cardboard base holding them is only a stand for the pieces. *From the Hugh A. Luck collection.*

WHISTLE, ca. 1920. Printed paper on curved board. This is a nice early figural Halloween noisemaker, 4.5 inches tall.

HORNS, ca. 1925. Painted pressed cardboard vegetable designs, made in Germany. 6.5 inches tall. *From the Hugh A. Luck collection.*

HORN, ca. 1920. "Crying Onion". Made in Germany, pressed paperboard. 5.5 inches high. *From the Chris J. Russell and the Halloween Queen collection.*

TAMBOURINE, ca. 1925. Lithographed tin with a kids and Jack-O'-Lantern design, made by Chein in the USA. 7 inches tall. *From the Hugh A. Luck collection.*

TAMBOURINE, ca. 1925. Lithographed tin with a cat design, made by Chein in the USA. 7 inches tall. *From the Hugh A. Luck collection.*

SQUEEKER, ca. 1930. Paperboard, German-made, 4.5 inches tall. *From the Chris J. Russell and the Halloween Queen collection.*

SQUEEZE TOY, ca. 1930. A lithographed cardboard accordion-style squeeze toy. It is German-made. 6 inches tall. *From the Hugh A. Luck collection.*

TAMBOURINE, ca. 1930. Lithographed paper over wooden frame. It is Japanese. 4 inches tall. *From the Hugh A. Luck collection.*

NOISEMAKER, ca. 1930. Made in the USA. Lithographed tin frying pan rattle.

NOISEMAKERS, ca. 1930. Celluloid head squeeker with a cloth body. Made in Germany. 6 inches high. *From the Chris J. Russell and the Halloween Queen collection.*

HORNS, ca. 1930. Lithographed paper tambourine-style horns, made in Germany. 8 inches tall. *From the Hugh A. Luck collection.*

NOISEMAKERS, ca. 1930. Made in the USA by J. Chien & Co. Lithographed tin tambourine and frying pan rattle. Chien was known for its high quality lithographed tin toys.

NOISEMAKERS, ca. 1930. Celluloid rattles with faces on both sides (happy & sad). Made in Germany. 4.5 inches high. *From the Chris J. Russell and the Halloween Queen collection.*

NOISEMAKER, ca. 1930. Lithographed tin tambourine.

HORN & DRUM RATTLE, ca. 1930. Lithographed tin with Jack-O'-Lantern design, made by T. Cohn in the USA. 11.5 inches tall. *From the Hugh A. Luck collection.*

TAMBOURINES, ca. 1940. Lithographed tin with a devil and a Dennison "witch in clouds" design, probably made by Chein or T. Cohn in the USA. 6 inches tall. *From the Chris J. Russell and the Halloween Queen collection.*

SQUEEKER, ca. 1935. A lithographed cardboard accordion-style squeeze toy. It is made in Boston. 3 inches tall. *From the Chris J. Russell and the Halloween Queen collection.*

TAMBOURINES, ca. 1940. Lithographed tin with cat designs, made in the USA. 7 inches and 6 inches tall. *From the Chris J. Russell and the Halloween Queen collection.*

NOISEMAKER, ca. 1945. Made in the USA by Merri-Lee. Decorated cardboard skeleton rattle.

TAMBOURINE, ca. 1940. Lithographed tin with a Jack-O'-Lantern design, probably made by Chein or T. Cohn in the USA. 6 inches tall. *From the Hugh A. Luck collection.*

SHAKER, ca. 1940. Decorated tin noisemaker with a wooden handle made in the USA. 4 inches tall. *From the Hugh A. Luck collection.*

NOISEMAKERS, ca. 1945. Rattles on a stick. *From the Chris J. Russell and the Halloween Queen collection.*

CYMBALS, ca. 1945. Lithographed tin with traditional design, made in the USA. 5.5 inches tall. *From the Hugh A. Luck collection.*

JESTER RATCHET, ca. 1955. Hard plastic noisemaker with a whistle handle in Halloween colors made in the USA. 6 inches tall. *From the Hugh A. Luck collection.*

NOISEMAKERS, ca. 1950. Lithographed tin rattles with Halloween designs and wooden handles. 3.5 inches across. Made by T. Cohn, Inc.

NOISEMAKERS, 1930-1960. Tin and paper noisemakers from the U.S., Japan, and Germany.

costumes, hats and masks

PARTY HAT, ca.1915. Made in Germany of lithographed paper.

PHOTO, 1915. A photo postcard of a girl in Halloween costume.

LURCH OF THE ADDAMS FAMILY, ca.1964. This is a tough-to-find costume of a favorite Addams Family character. To add spice to a simple costume, they added an image of Thing, the hand.

COSTUMES, 1916. From the Dennison *Bogie Book*.

PARTY HAT, ca. 1918. Elves rolling pumpkins made of crepe paper, by Dennison.

COSTUME, 1917. From the Dennison *Bogie Book*.

PARTY HAT, ca. 1918. Rats on pumpkins made of crepe paper with the addition of a flap at top in the shape of a cat's head.

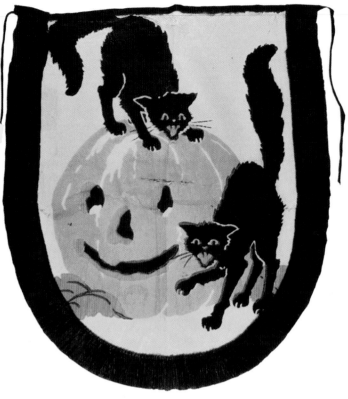

PARTY APRON, ca. 1918. Cats on pumpkins made of sewn crepe paper about 22 inches long, by Dennison.

PARTY APRON, ca. 1918. Cloud effect with witches made of sewn crepe paper about 22 inches long, by Dennison.

PARTY APRON, ca. 1918. White cats and pumpkin made of sewn crepe paper about 22 inches long, by Dennison.

PARTY APRON, ca. 1918. Witch in front of the moon made of sewn crepe paper about 22 inches long, probably by Dennison.

PARTY APRON, ca. 1918. Smiling Jack-O'-Lantern made of sewn crepe paper about 22 inches long, by Dennison.

PARTY HAT, ca. 1920. An unusual pumpkin hat made of crepe paper 14 inches tall. This hat was large enough to be pulled over a scarecrow's head.

PARTY APRON, ca. 1918. Owl and bats made of sewn crepe paper about 22 inches long, by Dennison.

PARTY HAT, ca. 1920. Made in USA of crepe paper.

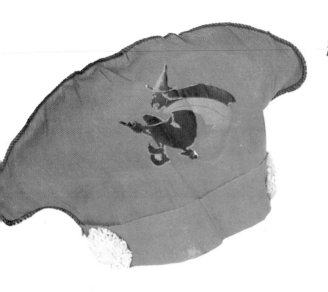

PARTY HATS, ca. 1920. Made by Dennison in USA of sewn crepe paper.

COSTUME, ca. 1920. The outfit is a Dennison's paper costume on the larger figure and a ca. 1938 home-made cloth costume on the smaller figure. *From the Chris J. Russell and the Halloween Queen collection.*

COSTUME, ca. 1920. The outfit is a Dennison's paper costume. *From the Chris J. Russell and the Halloween Queen collection.*

PHOTO, 1920s. Photos of kid in
Halloween clown costume with a
Jack-O'-Lantern.

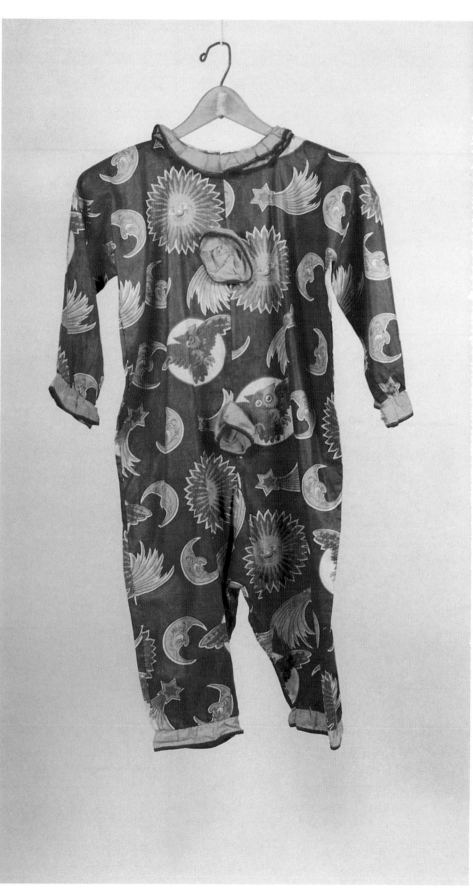

COSTUME, ca. 1920. A homemade clown costume with owls,
moons, comets and suns.

from Decorated Crepe No. H833.
Fringed Costume: The skirt is of crepe paper fringe. Plain waist and draped sash. The hat boasts no crown other than a wide double ruffle of orange crepe. The brim of the hat is Black Mat Stock No. 12.

COSTUMES, 1921. From the Dennison *Bogie Book*.

COSTUMES, 1922. From the Dennison *Bogie Book*.

COSTUMES, 1923. From the Dennison *Bogie Book.*

COSTUME, 1922. A Dennison children's cat costume made of crepe paper.

PHOTO, ca. 1923. A real photo of a Halloween party at the Calathusian Club.

COSTUMES, 1924. From the Dennison *Bogie Book.*

MASK, ca. 1925. Smiling cat face.

COSTUMES, 1925. From the Dennison *Bogie Book.*

PARTY HATS, ca. 1925. Made in Germany of paper. One shows dancing Jack-O'-Lanterns and the other shows cats, owl and Jack-O'-Lantern. These hats are made of a very thin paper. Also shown is a 1920s decorated paper doily.

COSTUMES, 1926. From the Dennison *Bogie Book*.

COSTUMES, 1927. From the Dennison *Party Magazine*.

PHOTO, 1930. A photo of a children's Halloween party.

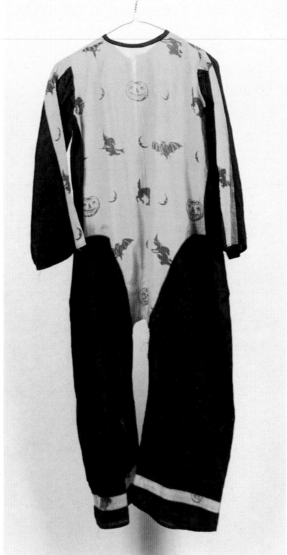

COSTUME, ca. 1930. A homemade Halloween costume that may have originally had a papier mache Jack-O'-Lantern mask.

COSTUME, ca. 1930. The box appears to be an early Collegeville costume box. It contained an Uncle Sam outfit.

PARTY HAT, ca. 1930. Made in USA of decorated crepe paper.

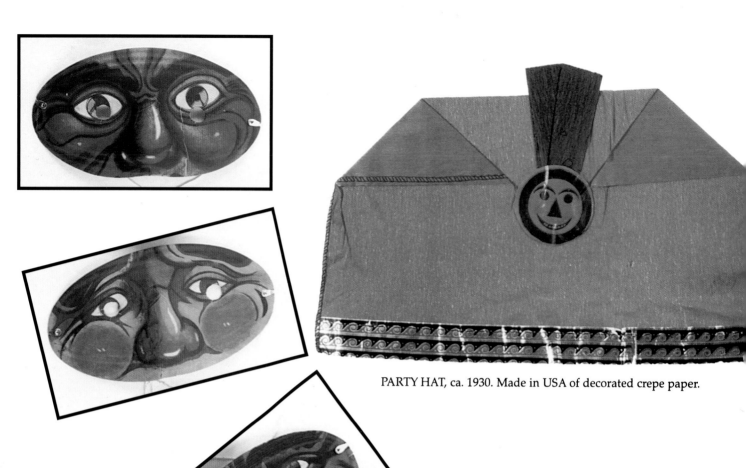

PARTY HAT, ca. 1930. Made in USA of decorated crepe paper.

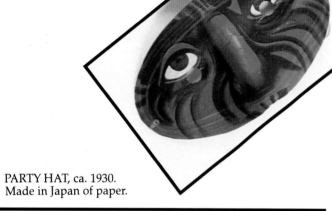

MASKS, ca. 1930. Paper masks for children, marked "Foreign Made". These may have been made in Japan.

PARTY HAT, ca. 1930.
Made in Japan of paper.

PARTY HAT, ca. 1930. Made in Japan of paper, 14 inches tall.

PARTY HATS, ca. 1935. Hats made of lithographed honeycomb tissue insert. Fairy hat made by Beistle. marked "Japan".

PARTY HATS, ca. 1935. Hats made of lithographed paper with honeycomb tissue insert. Fairy hat made by Beistle. Moon cat marked "Japan".

COSTUME, ca. 1938. A nice commercially made costume.

COSTUME, ca. 1940. A homemade Halloween dress.

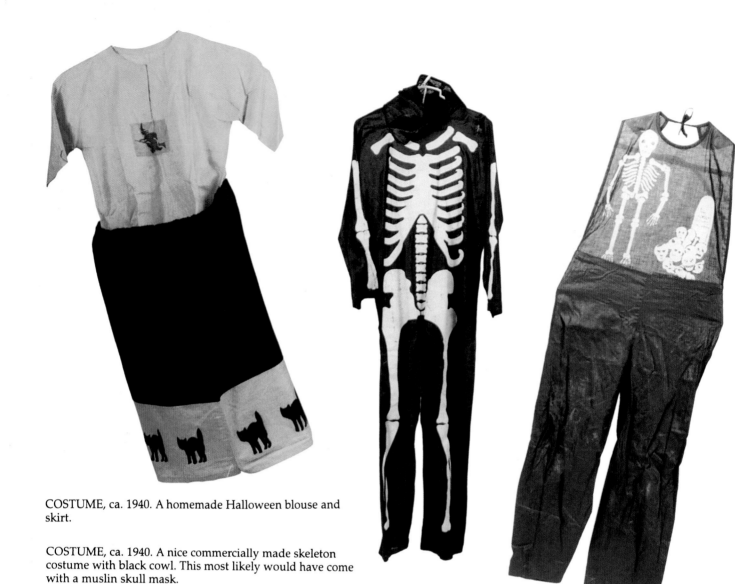

COSTUME, ca. 1940. A homemade Halloween blouse and skirt.

COSTUME, ca. 1940. A nice commercially made skeleton costume with black cowl. This most likely would have come with a muslin skull mask.

COSTUME, ca. 1942. A skeleton costume with a decided World War II propaganda message. On the tombstone are the names, Adolf, Benito, and Hirohito.

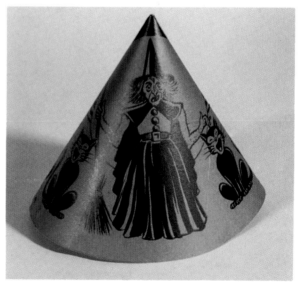

PARTY HAT, ca. 1940. Witch reading in moon. Made in USA of paper and honeycomb tissue.

PARTY HAT, ca. 1940. Witch with cats. Made of cardboard.

COSTUME, ca. 1945. The black witch's dress is handmade and decorated with embroidered cats, Jack-O'-Lanterns, spiders, and other Halloween images. *From the Chris J. Russell and the Halloween Queen collection.*

PARTY HATS, ca. 1945. These various hats are modeled by Longfellow, a 12 tall Steiff bear. Made in USA.

PARTY HAT, ca. 1945. This handsome pointed hat is modeled by Pierre an 18 inch tall bear. Made in USA.

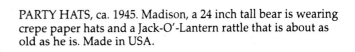

PARTY HATS, ca. 1945. Madison, a 24 inch tall bear is wearing crepe paper hats and a Jack-O'-Lantern rattle that is about as old as he is. Made in USA.

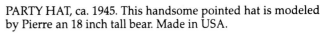

COSTUME, ca. 1950. Typical Collegeville costume box. It contained a pumpkin man outfit with a full head covering muslin mask.

PHOTO, 1953. Photos of the author and his sister in Halloween costumes.

PARTY HAT, ca. 1953. Black ghost escaping the flames. Made of cardboard.

PHOTO, 1953 & 1954. Photos of kids in Halloween costumes.

COSTUME, ca. 1956. Collegeville costume of Bugs Bunny with a full head covering cowl with ears and a muslin mask.

COSTUME, ca. 1958. A Ben Cooper Disney Tinkerbell costume with a thin plastic one piece mask.

COSTUME, ca. 1950. A devil costume perfect for the youngster who gives you a devil of a hard time.

PHOTO, 1955. Photos of kids in Halloween costumes.

COSTUME, ca. 1970. A Bland Charnas costume box containing a spaceman costume with a thin plastic mask. This costume is all vinyl with a silk-screened design. Children's costumes were quickly becoming nothing more than vinyl aprons with a mask and design on the vinyl.

COSTUME, ca. 1969. A Collegeville costume box containing a "First Man on the Moon" costume with a thin plastic mask.

COSTUME, ca. 1958. A Zorro costume box containing a thin plastic one piece mask. Probably made by Ben Cooper.

COSTUME, ca. 1962. A Ben Cooper costume box containing an astronaut costume with a thin plastic mask.

COSTUME, ca. 1989. A Ghostbuster II costume and accessories.

COSTUME, ca. 1962. A Halco costume box containing an astronaut costume with a thin plastic mask.

GIBSON, ca. 1908. Four cards published by Gibson and drawn by H.B. Griggs. *From the Chris J. Russell and the Halloween Queen collection.*

TUCK, ca. 1908. Eight cards published by Tuck with Halloween images that are reflected in the German candy containers. Printed in Germany. *From the Chris J. Russell and the Halloween Queen collection.*

AMERICAN POST CARD CO, ca. 1909. Two postcards, one illustration by Bernhardt Wall. The other is an unknown. *From the Hugh A. Luck collection.*

VALENTINE & SONS, ca. 1909. Two postcards, illustrations by Bernhardt Wall. Printed in Great Britain. *From the Hugh A. Luck collection.*

LUBRIE & ELKINS, ca. 1909-1915. Four cards published by Lubrie & Elkins with great Halloween images. *From the Chris J. Russell and the Halloween Queen collection.*

UNKNOWN, ca. 1910. Five cards showing Christmas type ornaments on Halloween. Was there a Halloween tree? The same card could have been offered at Christmas and Valentine's day with different captions. This particular set is very hard to find. *From the Chris J. Russell and the Halloween Queen collection.*

TUCK, ca. 1910. Five cards drawn by Frances Brundage of children doing Halloween things. Published by Tuck. The quality of the artwork is exceptional. *From the Chris J. Russell and the Halloween Queen collection.*

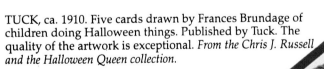

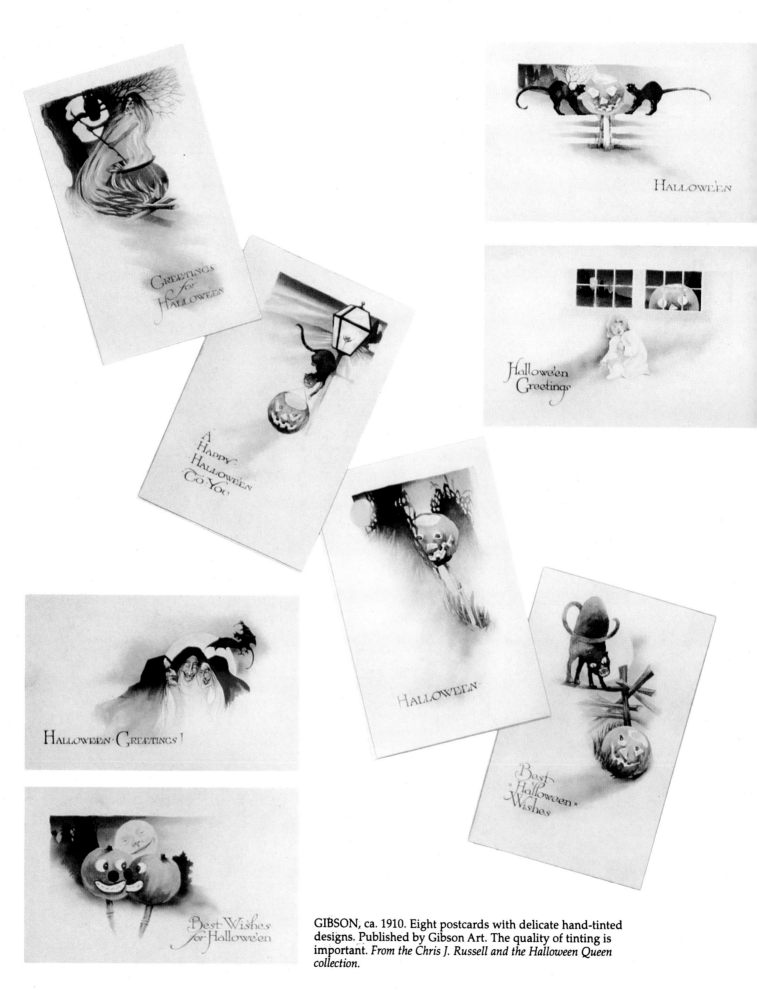

GIBSON, ca. 1910. Eight postcards with delicate hand-tinted designs. Published by Gibson Art. The quality of tinting is important. *From the Chris J. Russell and the Halloween Queen collection.*

WHITNEY, ca. 1910. Eight postcards with the vegetable figures that are sought after in candy container designs. Published by Whitney. *From the Chris J. Russell and the Halloween Queen collection.*

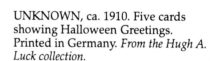

VALENTINE & SONS, ca. 1910. Three postcards, two illustrations by Bernhardt Wall. Printed in Great Britain. *From the Hugh A. Luck collection.*

VALENTINE & SONS, ca. 1910. A great illustration by an unknown artist. Printed in Great Britain. *From the Hugh A. Luck collection.*

UNKNOWN, ca. 1910. Five cards showing Halloween Greetings. Printed in Germany. *From the Hugh A. Luck collection.*

WOLF, ca. 1910. Two postcards published by Wolf Publishing (They used the lion's head symbol on the writing side). *From the Hugh A. Luck collection.*

UNKNOWN, ca. 1910. Nine cards showing Halloween pastimes and lots of great Jack-O'-Lanterns. Printed in Germany. *From the Hugh A. Luck collection.*

POSTCARDS, ca. 1911. Four cards printed in Germany. *From the Chris J. Russell and the Halloween Queen collection.*

POSTCARDS, ca. 1911.

POSTCARDS, ca. 1911.
Great pumpkin head kids.

POSTCARDS, ca. 1911. Images of children bobbing for apples, finding a cabbage root to tell one's fortune and a witch looking in her book of spells.

POSTCARDS, ca. 1911. Designs by Ellen Clapsaddle. Clapsaddle images often show smiling children.

POSTCARD, ca. 1911. Ghostly scarecrow with Jack-O'-Lantern head.

WINSCH, ca. 1911-1912. Four postcards by one of the most collectible publishers. John Winsch hired the finest illustrators and often combined works of two or more artists on one card. The illustrations were done by Schmucker. Printed in Germany. *From the Hugh A. Luck collection.*

WINSCH, ca. 1911. Four postcards by Winsch. Illustrations by Samuel L. Schmucker. Printed in Germany. *From the Hugh A. Luck collection.*

POSTCARD, ca. 1911. Cats in balloons.

UNKNOWN, ca. 1912. One showing a Halloween prank. The second card is published by Gottshulk & Dreyfuss. Both printed in Germany. *From the Hugh A. Luck collection.*

UNKNOWN, ca. 1911. Kids afraid of a Jack-O'-Lantern and a cat and playing games. Printed in Germany. *From the Hugh A. Luck collection.*

WINSCH, ca. 1912. Two postcards by Winsch. The one on the left is by an anonymous German artist while the other is a compilation of several artists. Printed in Germany. *From the Hugh A. Luck collection.*

WINSCH, ca. 1912 & 1914. Two postcards by Winsch. The top one is drawn by Schmucker. Printed in Germany. *From the Hugh A. Luck collection.*

WINSCH, ca. 1912. A postcard by Winsch. Illustrations by an anonymous German artist. Printed in Germany. *From the Hugh A. Luck collection.*

WOLF, ca. 1912 & 1915. Two postcards published by Wolf Publishing. *From the Hugh A. Luck collection.*

WINSCH, ca. 1913. Two postcards by Winsch. Illustrations by an anonymous German artist. Printed in Germany. *From the Hugh A. Luck collection.*

WINSCH, 1912. Four postcards by Winsch. Illustrations by an artist named Schmucker. Printed in Germany. *From the Hugh A. Luck collection.*

UNKNOWN, ca. 1912. Three postcards with wonderful witch images. Printed in Germany. *From the Hugh A. Luck collection.*

LUBRIE & ELKINS, ca. 1913. Four cards published by Lubrie & Elkins and drawn by H.B. Griggs with great Halloween images. *From the Chris J. Russell and the Halloween Queen collection.*

TUCK, ETC., ca. 1913. On the left are two postcards by Tuck. Illustrations by Schmucker. The card on the right is a Whitney-Schmuker of Worcester, Massachusetts. Printed in USA. *From the Hugh A. Luck collection.*

WINSCH, 1913. Four postcards by Winsch. It is believed that these illustrations were done by an artist named Schmucker. The quality of printing at this time was only obtainable in Germany. *From the Hugh A. Luck collection.*

WINSCH, ca. 1914 & 1913. Two postcards by Winsch. Artists unknown. Printed in Germany. *From the Hugh A. Luck collection.*

WINSCH, ca. 1913. Two postcards, one by Winsch. Illustration is a variation of earlier Schmuckers. The other is an unknown embossed card with a great illustration. Printed in Germany. *From the Hugh A. Luck collection.*

WOLF, ca. 1914. Published by Wolf Publishing. *From the Hugh A. Luck collection.*

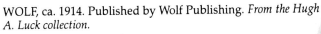

WINSCH, ca. 1914. Two postcards, one by Winsch. Illustration by Jason Freixas. The other is an unknown card with a great illustration. Printed in Germany. *From the Hugh A. Luck collection.*

WINSCH, 1914. Four postcards by Winsch. These illustrations were done by an unknown artist. Printed in Germany. *From the Hugh A. Luck collection.*

WINSCH, ca. 1915. Three postcards by Winsch. The children were done by an artist named Freixas, the backgrounds are Schmuckers. Printed in Germany. *From the Hugh A. Luck collection.*

WINSCH, ca. 1916. Three postcards by Winsch. The top illustration was done by artists Freixas & Schmuker, the other two are unknown mixtures. Printed in Germany. *From the Hugh A. Luck collection.*

CLAPSADDLE, ca. 1917. Two cards published by International Art Publishing. *From the Chris J. Russell and the Halloween Queen collection.*

WHITNEY, ca. 1917. Six postcards with the chubby cheeked kids. Published by Whitney. *From the Chris J. Russell and the Halloween Queen collection.*

POSTCARDS, ca. 1926. A series of eight cards designed by E.B. Weaver.

74

PARTY PLATES, ca. 1915 and 1950.

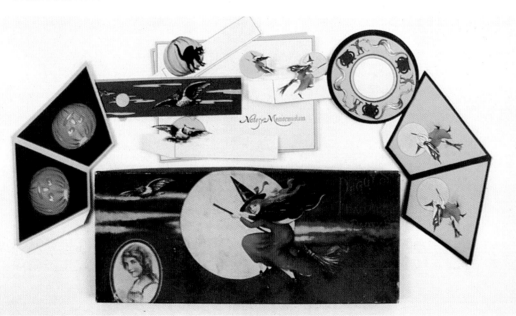

PARTY KIT, ca. 1915. Peggy's Halloween Party Box contains lamp shade covers, coasters, place cards, invitations. *From the Chris J. Russell and the Halloween Queen collection.*

CANDY DISH DECORATION, ca. 1915-1925. Small items, an inch to several inches tall would be stuck in a candy dish. The Jack-O'-Lantern boy with blue bells is a fortune telling favor that would have been stuck in a folded card. The fortune is on the back.

TABLE FAVORS, ca. 1915-1920. The paper owl had a fortune written on its lower half. The wing of the bat moved to reveal a stunt.

DOILY, ca. 1920. A nice accessory for the table decoration. It would have been the base for a candle stand or perhaps a candy dish.

PARTY KIT, ca. 1917. Dennison's Halloween Lunch Set would contain all the items necessary to have a Halloween luncheon. *From the Chris J. Russell and the Halloween Queen collection.*

TABLE FAVORS, ca. 1920. These paper items were available in a party book. They would be punched out and assembled. The book also contained invitations and place cards.

24 FORTUNE VERSES

WRAP EACH FORTUNE IN WAX PAPER AND BAKE IN HALLOWE'EN CAKE SO EACH PERSON WILL HAVE ONE

OR

TWIST EACH FORTUNE IN TINFOIL, PLACE IN WATER PAIL, FILL PAIL FULL OF WATER AND INVITE EVERYONE TO TAKE THE "FATAL PLUNGE".

MANY OTHER USES WILL SUGGEST THEMSELVES. INVALUABLE FOR PARTY USE.

JUST WHAT YOU ARE LOOKING FOR

FORTUNE VERSES, ca. 1922. Made in USA. The envelope contained slips of paper similar to those found in Chinese fortune cookies.

SERVIETTE, ca. 1920. Serviette means napkin in French, but this item was meant to act as a place mat or similar accessory. About 18 inches wide.

PLACE CARDS, ca. 1922. Made in USA by Dennison. Dennison's quality is exceptional.

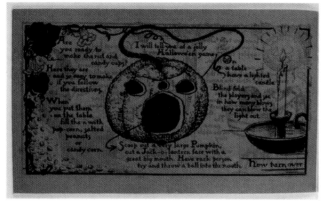

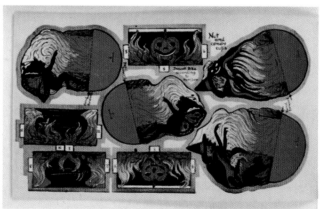

PARTY SET, ca. 1925. This party book came with invitations, lamp shades, table place tags, candle holder decorations and instructions. Individually, the pieces can be found, but finding the complete book is a great find. It was also available in an envelope. Made by Beistle. *From the Hugh A. Luck collection.*

PLACE CARDS, ca. 1925. Printed on thick paper, these cards were designed for the more formal party such as a bridge party or sit down dinner. Made in USA, maker unknown.

BRIDGE TALLIES, ca. 1930. Made in USA by RustCraft. Bridge parties were popular and the idea of a theme party, such as Halloween, was very appealing.

PLACE CARD, ca. 1925. Cute card that when held up to the light showed an old hag in the frame. Made in USA.

BRIDGE TALLIES, ca. 1925. Made in USA.

PLACE CARDS, ca. 1930. Made in USA, maker unknown.

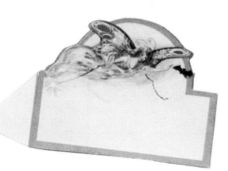

PLACE CARDS, ca. 1930. Made in USA, maker unknown.

PARTY SET, ca. 1930. Two cats and pumpkins on four napkins and a table cover. Possibly made by Reed for a bridge party. Made in USA.

PARTIGRAM, ca. 1930. A nice touch to a party. The host gave a few of these out during the party with great fanfare and everyone got a laugh.

PARTY SET, ca. 1930. A cat and pumpkins on four napkins and a table cover. Possibly made by Reed for a bridge party. Made in USA.

PARTY PLATE, ca. 1930.

TABLE COVER, ca. 1930. Masked pumpkins, made by C.A. Reed & Co.

NAPKINS, ca. 1930. Made by C.A. Reed & Co.

PARTY KIT, ca. 1936. Whitman's party set was probably aimed at kid's parties. *From the Chris J. Russell and the Halloween Queen collection.*

CANDY CUPS, 1940-1950. Candy cups went next to each plate on the table. These are probably Dennison as the stickers are their designs.

NAPKINs, ca. 1940 & 1950.
Made by C.A. Reed & Co.

PARTY PLATE &
NAPKIN, ca. 1950.

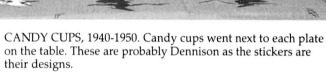

PARTY PLATE, ca. 1950. Made by Beach Products.

PARTY PLATE, ca. 1950.

Decorations

STREAMERS, ca. 1913. Made by Dennison.

CREPE PAPER, ca. 1914. Witches on Flying Machines. 20 inches wide by 10 feet long. A nice early image incorporating the latest invention - The Flying Machine.

CREPE PAPER, ca. 1912. Yellow Pumpkins On Black. 20 inches wide by 10 feet long. Made by Dennison, pattern #988

DECORATION, ca. 1915. Interesting hanging decoration. Made of handpainted hollow board disks, a quarter of an inch thick. Made in Germany. 3 inches wide. *From the Chris J. Russell and the Halloween Queen collection.*

CREPE PAPER, ca. 1916. Two variations on a design with the black & white design coming a few years before the orange variation. 12 inches wide by 10 feet long. Made by American Tissue Mills.

CREPE PAPER, ca. 1916. Ghost and witches tug-of-war. 20 inches wide by 10 feet long. Made by Dennison.

CREPE PAPER, ca. 1916. Witches in the Sky. 20 inches wide by 10 feet long. Probably made by Dennison.

CREPE PAPER, ca. 1916. 20 inches wide by 10 feet long. Made by American Tissue Mills.

CREPE PAPER, ca. 1916. Witches with Jack-O'-Lanterns. 20 inches wide by 10 feet long. Made by Dennison #854

SILHOUETTES, ca. 1916. Silhouettes made by Beistle in USA.

CREPE PAPER, ca. 1918. Pumpkin Men By The Fence. 20 inches wide by 10 feet long. Unknown maker. *From the Chris J. Russell and the Halloween Queen collection.*

CREPE PAPER, ca. 1916. Three owls. 20 inches wide by 10 feet long.

SILHOUETTES, ca. 1916. Cats made by Dennison. These could be used alone as a wall decoration or glued to other items to create candy containers or other things.

CREPE PAPER, ca. 1918. Dancing banjo playing cat and pumpkin. 19 inches by 18 inches wide. This is a portion of 10 foot roll.

CREPE PAPER BORDER, ca. 1918. Witch and cauldron. 8.5 inches wide by 10 feet long.

CREPE PAPER, ca. 1918. White cats and pumpkin by Dennison. 20 inches by 10 feet long. Pattern #H856

CREPE PAPER BORDER, ca. 1918. Pumpkin man with cats, 6.5 inches wide by 10 feet long. A Dennison's product.

CREPE PAPER, ca. 1918. Singing cats and witches. 20 inches wide by 10 feet long. Probably made by Dennison.

CREPE PAPER BORDER, ca. 1918. Pumpkins, 8.5 inches wide by 10 feet long. A Dennison's product.

WALL DECORATION, ca. 1918. Die cut sax-playing pumpkin girl. 4.25 inches tall. German-made. *From the Chris J. Russell and the Halloween Queen collection.*

CREPE PAPER, ca. 1918. Black cats and pumpkin by Dennison. 20 inches by 10 feet. Pattern #H852

CREPE PAPER, ca. 1920. Witch Above The Tree Tops. 20 inches wide by 10 feet long. Unknown maker. *From the Chris J. Russell and the Halloween Queen collection.*

LADIES HOME JOURNAL, 1919. Decorating ideas for the home using Dennison's crepe papers and loads of creativity.

CREPE PAPER, ca. 1920. Black cats and bats. 20 inches wide by 10 feet long. Unknown maker. *From the Chris J. Russell and the Halloween Queen collection.*

STREAMERS, ca. 1916 and 1930. The lower one made by Dennison.

89

GUMMED SEALS, ca. 1920s Made by Gibson Publishing. *From the Chris J. Russell and the Halloween Queen collection.*

GUMMED SEALS, ca. 1920s Made by Dennison. *From the Chris J. Russell and the Halloween Queen collection.*

DECORATIONS, ca. 1920. The owl looks like the typical Christmas tree decoration. Halloween decorations were also made and hung from lights and on walls. For Halloween, you could replace your Christmas bulbs with Halloween bulbs and light up a doorway or cornstalk. 2 inches and 3 inches tall. *From the Chris J. Russell and the Halloween Queen collection.*

WALL DECORATION, ca. 1920. A die cut pumpkin man. Multi-color lithographed paper probably made in Germany. 21 inches tall.

WALL DECORATION, ca. 1920. A die cut pumpkin man. Embossed pressed paper probably made in Germany. 18 inches tall.

WALL DECORATION, ca. 1920. A die cut cat on the moon. Embossed pressed paper probably made in Germany. 13 inches tall.

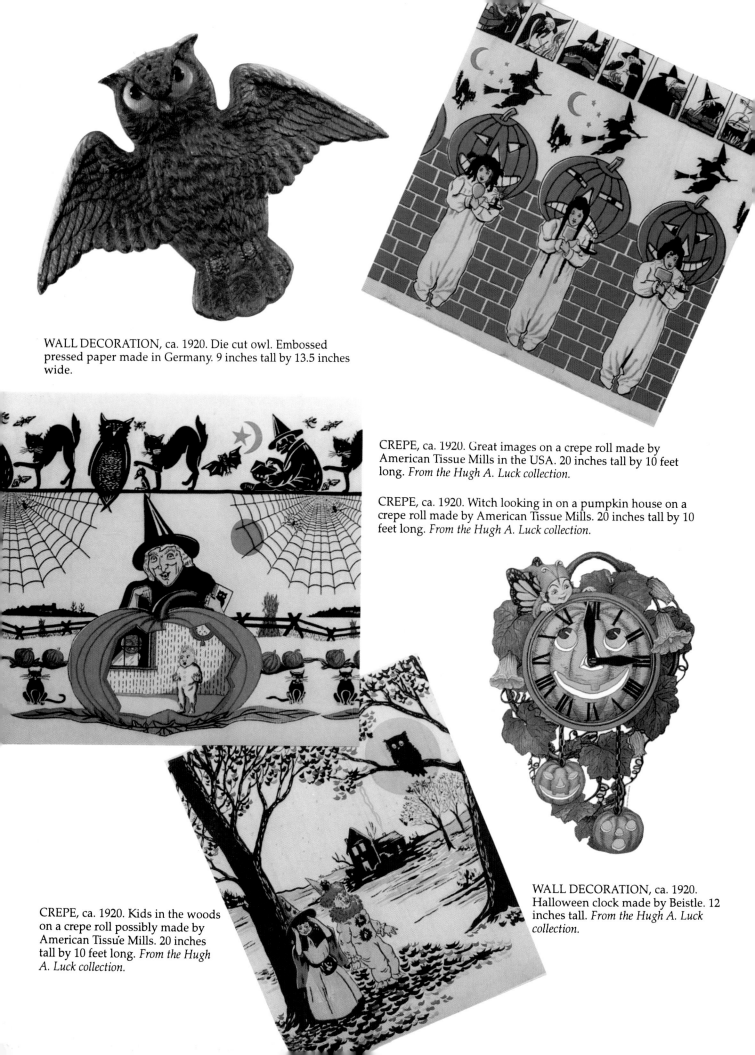

WALL DECORATION, ca. 1920. Die cut owl. Embossed pressed paper made in Germany. 9 inches tall by 13.5 inches wide.

CREPE, ca. 1920. Great images on a crepe roll made by American Tissue Mills in the USA. 20 inches tall by 10 feet long. *From the Hugh A. Luck collection.*

CREPE, ca. 1920. Witch looking in on a pumpkin house on a crepe roll made by American Tissue Mills. 20 inches tall by 10 feet long. *From the Hugh A. Luck collection.*

CREPE, ca. 1920. Kids in the woods on a crepe roll possibly made by American Tissue Mills. 20 inches tall by 10 feet long. *From the Hugh A. Luck collection.*

WALL DECORATION, ca. 1920. Halloween clock made by Beistle. 12 inches tall. *From the Hugh A. Luck collection.*

WALL DECORATION, ca. 1920. A die cut garland of cats printed on a cheap board paper.

CREPE PAPER, ca. 1920. Witches. 20 inches wide by 10 feet long. Made by Bainbridge.

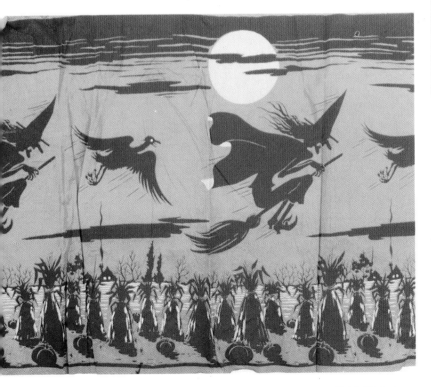

CREPE PAPER, ca. 1920. Witch above a cornfield. 20 inches wide by 10 feet long. Unknown maker. *From the Chris J. Russell and the Halloween Queen collection.*

CREPE PAPER, ca. 1920. Jack-O'-Lantern hot air balloon. 20 inches wide by 10 feet long. Unknown maker. *From the Chris J. Russell and the Halloween Queen collection.*

WALL DECORATION, ca. 1920. A die cut Jack-O'-Lantern. 7 inches tall. Printed on a cheap board paper, these items are very brittle.

LAMP DECORATION, ca. 1920. Die cut faux stained glass window of paper board and colored tissue. 12 inches tall. An exceptional Halloween decoration.

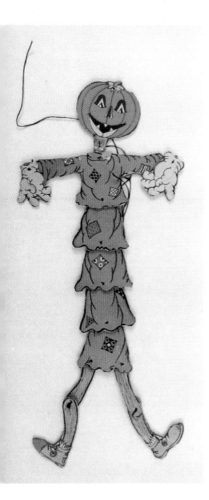

WALL DECORATION, ca. 1920. A die cut garland printed on a cheap board paper.

WALL DECORATION, ca. 1922. Die cut jointed pumpkin man. 14 inches tall. *From the Chris J. Russell and the Halloween Queen collection.*

CREPE PAPER, ca. 1922. Elves and witches. 20 inches wide by 10 feet long. Probably made by Dennison.

WALL DECORATION, ca. 1920. Embossed paper board with bloodcurdling skeleton in graveyard scene. 19 inches tall. An exceptional Halloween decoration.

WALL DECORATION, ca. 1920. Die cut cat. Embossed pressed paper made in Germany. 19.5 inches tall. *From the Chris J. Russell and the Halloween Queen collection.*

TABLE DECORATION, ca. 1920. A die cut pumpkin head figure fence printed on board paper. This could have been used as part of a center-piece. Each are 5.5 inches tall.

CREPE PAPER BORDER, ca. 1922. Dennison's paper 6 inches wide by 10 feet long.

CREPE PAPER DECORATION, in the style of the 1920s. Dennison's Bogie Books show hanging decorations made by pasting crepe to cardboard, then cutting out the design and adding silhouettes and other decoration. This is a good use of damaged crepe paper that doesn't display well by itself.

CREPE PAPER, ca. 1925. Witch with Jack-O'-Lantern. 20 inches wide by 10 feet long. Made by Perkins Paper, a division of American Tissue Mills, Holyoke, Massachusetts.

FIGURES, ca. 1920-1945. The first two figures were made by Beistle. The second figure is mechanical. As you turn a dial at the bottom, the witch's hat goes up and down. Items 3 and 4 are Dennison's door knob decorations. All about 9 inches tall. *From the Hugh A. Luck collection.*

WALL DECORATION, ca. 1925.
Jointed lightening monster "Bug &
Wumpus" made by Beistle. 28 inches
tall. *From the Hugh A. Luck collection.*

WALL DECORATION, ca. 1925. Flat
paper witch and hands to be used as
part of a Dennison's "scene". About
30 inches. *From the Hugh A. Luck
collection.*

WALL DECORATION, ca. 1925.
Jointed lightening devil made by
Beistle. 28 inches tall. *From the Hugh
A. Luck collection.*

FIREPLACE SCREEN, ca. 1925.
Embossed paperboard figures on a
thinner orange paper backing. This 3
fold screen is an exceptional piece
that looks wonderful with back light.
Made in Germany. 26 inches wide by
19.5 inches tall. *From the Hugh A. Luck
collection.*

WALL DECORATION, ca. 1925. Embossed paperboard figure of a blackface man. Made in Germany. 16 inches wide. *From the Hugh A. Luck collection.*

WALL DECORATION, ca. 1925. Embossed paper board with witch, bat & cats. 19 inches tall. An exceptional Halloween decoration.

CREPE PAPER, ca. 1927. Pumpkin head Raggedy Ann & Andy in a field. 20 inches wide by 10 feet long. Unknown maker. *From the Chris J. Russell and the Halloween Queen collection.*

CREPE PAPER, ca. 1925. Goblins on the roof. 20 inches wide by 10 feet long. Unknown maker. *From the Chris J. Russell and the Halloween Queen collection.*

WALL DECORATION, ca. 1925-1931. Jointed crepe and paper bat made by Beistle. 21 inches wide. For such a popular Halloween figure, the bat appears less frequently as an individual decoration. *From the Hugh A. Luck collection.*

WALL DECORATION, ca. 1928. Honeycomb body witch made by Beistle. 24 inches tall.

WALL DECORATION, ca. 1928. Honeycomb body cat made by Beistle. 24 inches tall.

WALL DECORATION, ca. 1928. Die cut raised pressed cardboard pumpkin men that bear a resemblance to Mickey Mouse. About 7.5 inches tall. *From the Chris J. Russell and the Halloween Queen collection.*

WALL DECORATION, ca. 1928. Jointed mechanical witch made by Beistle. 18 inches tall. *From the Hugh A. Luck collection.*

GUMMED SEALS, ca. 1930s Made by Beistle. *From the Chris J. Russell and the Halloween Queen collection.*

TABLE COVER, ca. 1930. Halloween scene. 54 inches wide by 72 inches long. Made by Reed.

WALL DECORATION, ca. 1935. Embossed paperboard owl in moon made in Germany. 18 inches tall. *From the Hugh A. Luck collection.*

CREPE PAPER, ca. 1930. Pumpkin man pulling cart. 20 inches wide by 10 feet long. Made by Dennison.

TABLE DECORATION, ca. 1930. Honeycomb paper witch. 2.5 inches tall by 3 inches wide.

WALL DECORATION, ca. 1935. Embossed paperboard decorations and their original box, made in Germany. 15.5 inches tall. *From the Hugh A. Luck collection.*

WALL DECORATION, ca. 1935. Embossed paperboard cat musicians made in Germany. This is part of a series that was also made in a smaller size. 15 inches tall. *From the Hugh A. Luck collection.*

WALL DECORATIONS, ca. 1935. Embossed paperboard devils made in Germany. 15.5 inches to 20 inches tall. *From the Hugh A. Luck collection.*

WALL DECORATION, ca. 1935. Embossed paperboard Jack-O'-Lantern made by Beistle in the USA. 28 inches tall. *From the Hugh A. Luck collection.*

TABLE DECORATIONS, ca. 1935. Two exceptional Beistle honeycomb paper pieces. One is a Halloween game and the other is a candy holder. The one on the left is 11 inches tall. *From the Hugh A. Luck collection.*

WALL DECORATION, ca. 1935. Embossed paperboard skull & cross bones made in Germany. 10 inches tall. *From the Hugh A. Luck collection.*

WALL DECORATION, ca. 1935. Jointed crepe and paper ghost made in USA. 11.5 inches tall. *From the Hugh A. Luck collection.*

WALL DECORATION, ca. 1938. Die cut street cats. Embossed pressed paper made in USA. 12 inches tall.

WALL DECORATION, ca. 1938. Die cut jazz skeletons. Embossed pressed paper made in USA. 12 inches tall.

WALL DECORATION, ca. 1938. Die cut Stern cats. Embossed pressed paper made in USA. 12 inches tall.

WALL DECORATION, ca. 1938. Die cut crows on a scarecrow. Embossed pressed paper made in USA. 12 inches tall.

WALL DECORATION, ca. 1938. Die cut cat on a fence. Embossed pressed paper made in USA. This was part of a series in different colors. The silver is the toughest to find. 12 inches tall.

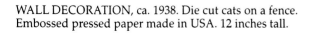

WALL DECORATION, ca. 1938. Die cut cats on a fence. Embossed pressed paper made in USA. 12 inches tall.

CREPE PAPER BORDER, ca. 1940.
6 inches wide by 10 feet long.

WALL DECORATION, ca. 1940. A die cut purple skeleton on a
straw mule. Printed flat, no embossing. 18 inches tall.

WALL DECORATION, ca. 1940. A die cut witch before her
cauldron. Printed flat, no embossing. 3.5 inches tall.

WALL DECORATION, ca. 1940. Embossed paperboard figure of a cat on a Jack-O'-Lantern. Made in U.S.A. 13 inches tall. *From the Hugh A. Luck collection.*

WALL DECORATION, ca. 1940. Embossed paperboard figure of a cat. 18.5 inches tall. *From the Hugh A. Luck collection.*

WALL DECORATION, ca. 1940. Embossed paperboard figure of a cat. This may be earlier than 1940. Made in U.S.A. 12 inches tall. *From the Hugh A. Luck collection.*

WALL DECORATION, ca. 1940. Embossed paperboard figure of a cat's head. This is a very popular figure available probably from the late 1930s to the 1950s. 11 inches wide.

WALL DECORATION, ca. 1945. Embossed paperboard figure of a cat head. Made in U.S.A. 12 inches tall. *From the Hugh A. Luck collection.*

WALL DECORATION, ca. 1947. Jointed paper bat made by Beistle. 18 inches wide. *From the Hugh A. Luck collection.*

WALL DECORATION, ca. 1947. Jointed skeleton Jumping Jack (legs and arms are strung together to so that whole figure will jump and jiggle) made by Beistle. 23 inches tall. *From the Hugh A. Luck collection.*

WALL DECORATION, ca. 1945. Flat paper jointed pumpkin man. 16 inches. Made in U.S.A.

WALL DECORATION, ca. 1945. Flat paper witch with crepe hair. 16 inches. Made in U.S.A. *From the Hugh A. Luck collection.*

TABLE DECORATION, ca. 1945. Black cat on honeycomb base. 9.5 inches tall. *From the Hugh A. Luck collection.*

WALL DECORATION, ca. 1949 - 1957. Jointed crepe and paper owl made by Beistle. 9 inches tall. *From the Hugh A. Luck collection.*

STAND UP DECORATION, ca. 1950. A die cut scarecrow. Printed flat, no embossing. 12 inches tall.

WALL DECORATION, ca. 1950. Jointed crepe and paper witch made by Beistle. 9 inches tall. *From the Hugh A. Luck collection.*

WALL DECORATION, ca. 1948. Embossed paperboard figure of a witch looking up at two mice on the brim of her hat. 18 inches tall. *From the Hugh A. Luck collection.*

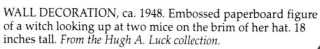

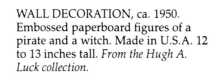

WALL DECORATION, ca. 1950. Embossed paperboard figures of a pirate and a witch. Made in U.S.A. 12 to 13 inches tall. *From the Hugh A. Luck collection.*

FAVORS, ca. 1950. Three tiny witches with brooms, about 3 inches tall, are made with composition heads and pipe cleaner bodies. They could have been used in a centerpiece or as a decoration on a cake. Made in Japan.

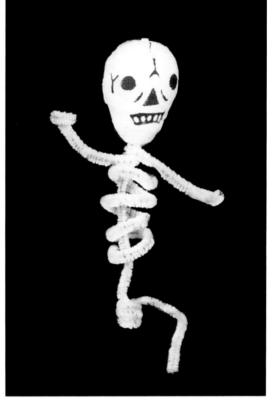

FAVOR, ca. 1950. Tiny skeleton about 3 inches tall. Papier mache head and pipe cleaner body. Made in Japan.

TABLE DECORATION, ca. 1950. A paper and honeycomb tissue scarecrow. 8 inches tall.

WALL DECORATION, ca. 1950. A die cut pirate owl. 10.5 inches tall. Made by Luhrs.

WALL DECORATION, ca. 1950. A die cut witch. 8 inches tall.

WALL DECORATION, ca. 1950. A die cut owl. 9 inches tall. Made by Luhrs.

WALL DECORATION, ca. 1950. A die cut Jack-O'-Lantern done with a shadow box effect. 9 inches tall.

WALL DECORATION, ca. 1950. A die cut jointed cat. 8 inches. Probably by Luhrs.

WALL DECORATION, ca. 1950. A die cut cat with Jack-O'-Lantern. 9 inches tall. Made by Luhrs.

WALL DECORATION, ca. 1950. A die cut Jack-O'-Lantern. 9 inches tall. Made by Luhrs.

WALL DECORATION, ca. 1950. A die cut witch. 10.5 inches tall. Made by Luhrs.

WALL DECORATION, ca. 1950. A die cut cat in a hat. 9 inches tall. Made by Luhrs.

WALL DECORATION, ca. 1950. A die cut cat in the moon. 14 inches tall. Made by Luhrs.

WALL DECORATION, ca. 1950. Die cut musical cats. 9 inches.
Made by Luhrs.

TABLE DECORATION, ca. 1950. A plastic cat and crescent
moon. 5.5 inches tall.

WALL DECORATION, ca. 1950. Die cut cat designs. 9 inches
wide. Possibly made by Luhrs.

CREPE PAPER BORDER, ca.
1950. 6.5 inches wide by 10 feet
long.

TABLE DECORATION, ca. 1950 - 1962. Black cat on honeycomb base. 12 inches tall. *From the Hugh A. Luck collection.*

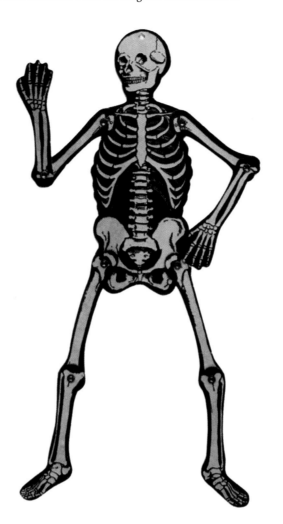

WALL DECORATION, ca. 1950. Die cut skeleton. Lithographed paper board made in USA. 18 inches tall. Skeletons were made by the millions and are still popular today. They can be found in all sizes, usually have movable joints and are sometimes painted with glow in the dark paint.

WALL DECORATION, ca. 1956 -1965. Jointed crepe and paper owl made by Beistle. 7.5 inches tall. *From the Hugh A. Luck collection.*

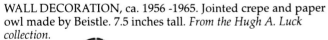

JOINTED FIGURES, ca. 1952. These are parts of popular sets made by Beistle in the USA in the 1940s and 1950s. 14 to 15 inches tall. *From the Hugh A. Luck collection.*

STICKERS, ca. 1950. Small 1 inch gummed stickers to attach to the envelopes of your Halloween cards and invitations.

CANDLES, ca. 1959. Here is a nice collection of Halloween figural candles.

LANTERNS, ca. 1912. Composition Jack-O'-Lanterns with tissue paper inserts. 3 inches tall, most likely made in Germany.

LANTERN, ca. 1890. "The Witch", delicate blown glass, made in Germany. 4.75 inches tall. Rare. *From the Chris J. Russell and the Halloween Queen collection.*

LANTERN, ca. 1915. "Upright Watermelon", composition with a glass nose, made in Germany. The glass nose adds extra value. 3.5 inches tall. *From the Chris J. Russell and the Halloween Queen collection.*

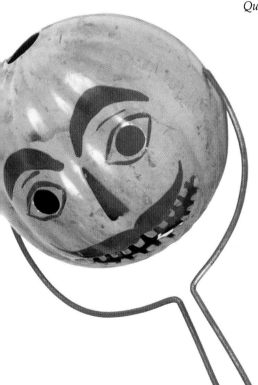

PARADE LANTERN, ca. 1908. Metal, hollow parade Jack-O'-Lantern. 6.5 inches high (not including handle). Made in Toledo, Ohio. *From the Chris J. Russell and the Halloween Queen collection.*

PARADE LANTERN, ca. 1908. Metal, hollow parade Jack-O'-Lantern. 6.5 inches high (not including handle). In use, would be attached to a pole. Made in Toledo, Ohio. *From the Chris J. Russell and the Halloween Queen collection.*

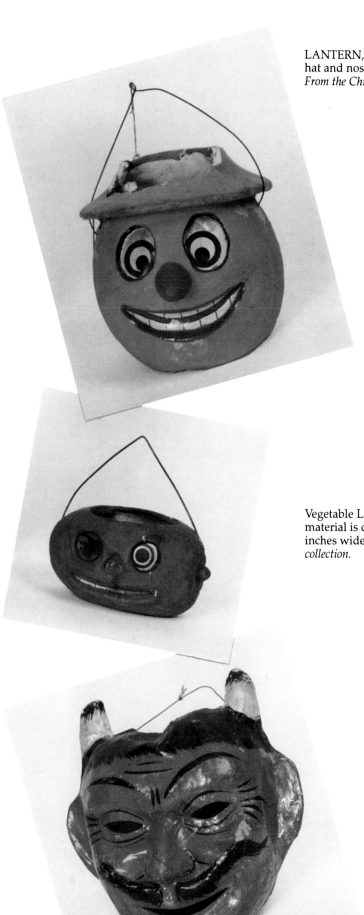

LANTERN, ca. 1916. An unusual early lantern with an applied hat and nose. Composition, made in Germany. 4.5 inches tall. *From the Chris J. Russell and the Halloween Queen collection.*

LANTERN, ca. 1920. Jack-O'-Lantern of formed paperboard. This one is done up as a clown face. Made in Germany. 4.5 inches tall. *From the Chris J. Russell and the Halloween Queen collection.*

Vegetable LANTERN, ca. 1916. A watermelon lantern. The material is composition. Made in Germany. 2 inches tall by 4 inches wide. *From the Chris J. Russell and the Halloween Queen collection.*

FOX LANTERN, ca. 1920. A brown fuzzy fox face lantern. The material is composition. Made in Germany. 3.75 inches tall. This is a very unusual lantern. *From the Chris J. Russell and the Halloween Queen collection.*

LANTERN, ca. 1916. Devil's head lantern of composition-covered formed paperboard. Made in Germany. 6 inches tall. *From the Chris J. Russell and the Halloween Queen collection.*

LANTERN, ca. 1920. "Humpty Dumpty", Pressed board with composition wash, made in Germany. 4.25 inches tall. *From the Chris J. Russell and the Halloween Queen collection.*

CAT LANTERN, ca. 1920. A black cat face lantern. The material is composition. Made in Germany. 4.75 inches tall.

CAT LANTERN, ca. 1920. A green fuzzy cat face lantern. The material is composition. Made in Germany. 2.5 inches tall. *From the Chris J. Russell and the Halloween Queen collection.*

BLACK CAT, ca. 1920. Pressed cardboard lantern with glossy paper inserts. German-made and 6.25 inches tall. *From the Hugh A. Luck collection.*

OWL, ca. 1920. Pressed cardboard lantern with tissue paper inserts. German-made and 5.75 inches tall. Owl lanterns are rare birds. *From the Hugh A. Luck collection.*

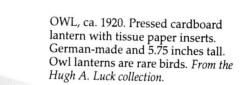

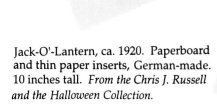

Jack-O'-Lantern, ca. 1920. Paperboard and thin paper inserts, German-made. 10 inches tall. *From the Chris J. Russell and the Halloween Collection.*

LANTERN, ca. 1920. Paperboard and thin paper. 8 inches tall. Made in Germany. This is an exceptionally colorful piece. *From the Chris J. Russell and the Halloween Queen collection.*

LANTERN, ca. 1920. Cardboard and thin paper. 6 inches tall. *From the Chris J. Russell and the Halloween Queen collection.*

LANTERN, ca. 1920. Paperboard and thin paper. 10 inches tall. *From the Chris J. Russell and the Halloween Queen collection.*

LANTERN, ca. 1920. Paperboard and thin paper. 11 inches tall. Each panel is different. *From the Chris J. Russell and the Halloween Queen collection.*

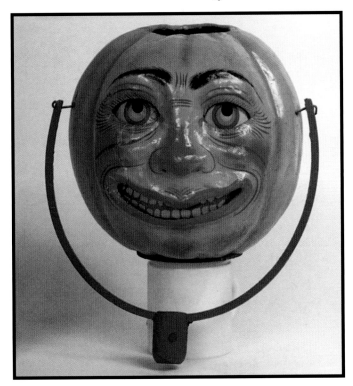

PARADE TORCH, ca. 1920. A fabulous layered papier mache lantern with torch handle and paper inserts. This is a very unusual piece and could be the centerpiece of any collection. German-made and 13 inches tall. *From the Hugh A. Luck collection.*

Jack-O'-Lantern, ca. 1920. A heavy composition lantern with composition bottom and paper inserts. A Chinese face, German-made and 4 inches tall. *From the Hugh A. Luck collection.*

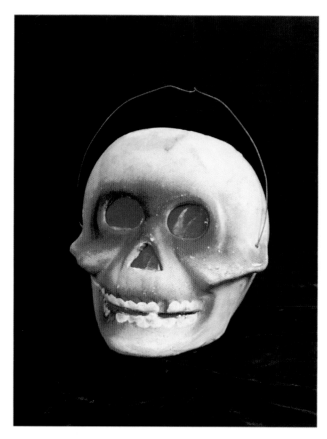

Jack-O'-Lantern, ca. 1920. Pressed cardboard lantern with crepe ears and paper inserts. German-made and 5 inches tall. It looks like a fish head but probably is an owl. *From the Hugh A. Luck collection.*

SKULL, ca. 1920. Composition lantern with red paper inserts. It is German-made. 4.5 inches tall. *From the Hugh A. Luck collection.*

WATERMELON, ca. 1920. Pressed cardboard lantern with paper inserts. German-made and 2.5 inches tall by 4.5 inches wide. These watermelon figures are very difficult to find. *From the Hugh A. Luck collection.*

BLACK CAT, ca. 1920. Pressed cardboard lantern with glossy paper inserts. German-made and 6.25 inches tall. *From the Hugh A. Luck collection.*

OWL LANTERN, ca. 1920. An owl lantern, made of pressed and formed paperboard. German. 4.5 inches tall.

LANTERN, ca. 1920. An eared Jack-O'-Lantern, made of pressed and formed paperboard. German. 6 inches tall.

LANTERNS, ca. 1920. Devil lanterns, composition, made in Germany. The lantern on the right shows the effect of being stored in a damp environment. 2.75 inches and 3.75 inches tall. *From the Chris J. Russell and the Halloween Queen collection.*

LANTERNS, ca. 1920. Formed paperboard and thin paper. Each of these simple Jack-O'-Lanterns have a personality of their own. 3 inches tall. *From the Chris J. Russell and the Halloween Queen collection.*

LANTERN, ca. 1920. Smiling devil of formed paperboard and thin paper. Made in Germany. 3 inches tall. *From the Chris J. Russell and the Halloween Queen collection.*

LANTERNS, ca. 1920. Black cats of formed paperboard and thin paper. Made in Germany. 3 inches tall. *From the Chris J. Russell and the Halloween Queen collection.*

LANTERN, ca. 1920. An incredible Jack-O'-Lantern cauldron on wire feet made of composition, German, 4 inches tall. *From .the Chris J. Russell and the Halloween Queen collection.*

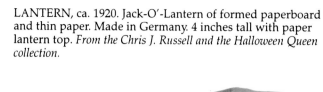

LANTERN, ca. 1920. Jack-O'-Lantern of formed paperboard and thin paper. Made in Germany. 4 inches tall with paper lantern top. *From the Chris J. Russell and the Halloween Queen collection.*

LANTERN, ca. 1920. Another great lantern in the shape of the head of a dog. It has personality and is in perfect condition. Composition, made in Germany. 4.5 inches tall. *From the Chris J. Russell and the Halloween Queen collection.*

LANTERN, ca. 1920. Jack-O'-Lantern of formed paperboard and thin paper. Made in Germany. 3 inches tall. There is a reflective coralene bead finish to the lantern. *From the Chris J. Russell and the Halloween Queen collection.*

LANTERN, ca. 1920. One horned Goblin lantern of composition, German, 3.5 inches tall. *From the Chris J. Russell and the Halloween Queen collection.*

LANTERN, ca. 1920. Devil head of formed paperboard. This one is great. It is complex, has personality and is in super condition. Made in Germany. 5.5 inches tall. *From the Chris J. Russell and the Halloween Queen collection.*

LANTERNS, ca. 1920. Jack-O'-Lantern scarecrow figure and owl's head lanterns of formed paperboard. The owl is very creative. It is complex, has personality and is in super condition. Made in Germany. 6 inches and 4.5 inches tall. *From the Chris J. Russell and the Halloween Queen collection.*

LANTERN, ca. 1920. Jack-O'-Lantern of formed paperboard. This is also a candy container that opens at the neck. Made in Germany. 6 inches tall. *From the Chris J. Russell and the Halloween Queen collection.*

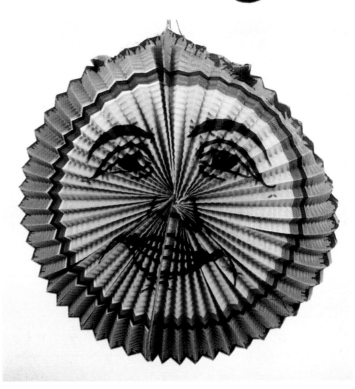

LANTERN, ca. 1920. Japanese-style paper lantern with Jack-O'-Lantern. 8.25 inches in diameter.

LANTERN, ca. 1920. Japanese-style paper lantern representing the man in the moon. 13 inches in diameter.

LANTERN, ca. 1922. Japanese-style paper lantern in the shape of a cat's head. 7.5 inches in diameter.

LANTERN, ca. 1922. Japanese-style paper lantern with cat and witch. 13 inches in diameter.

LANTERN, ca. 1924. Japanese-style paper lantern. 11 inches tall.

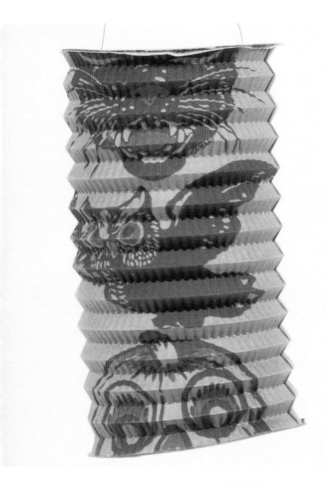 

LANTERN, ca. 1924. Japanese-style paper lantern. 8 inches tall.

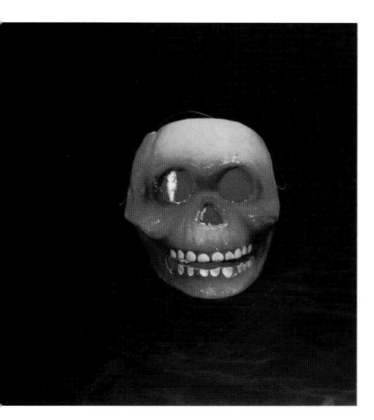 

LANTERN, ca. 1925. "Red Eye Skull", composition, made in Germany. 3.75 inches tall. *From the Chris J. Russell and the Halloween Queen collection.*

LANTERN, ca. 1925. Pressed cardboard. This is an exceptional addition to any collection. German-made. 2.75 inches tall. *From the Hugh A. Luck collection.*

LANTERNS, ca. 1925. Pressed and formed paperboard Jack-O'-Lanterns with tissue paper inserts. 4 inches, 7 inches and 3.5 inches tall, Made in Germany. This style was recreated in West Germany in the 1950s and the bottoms were marked "West Germany".

LANTERN, ca. 1925. This paperboard cat, bat & witch lantern with tissue inserts is folded flat. It came with a bottom circular piece that would hold the candle and the lantern in its round shape. 12 inches wide by 10 inches tall.

LANTERN & PIPE, ca. 1925. Pressed paperboard Jack-O'-Lantern and pipe made in Germany. Jack-O'-Lantern is 5.5 inches tall. *From the Hugh A. Luck collection.*

DEVIL LANTERN, ca. 1930. Pressed cardboard. German-made. 7 inches tall. *From the Hugh A. Luck collection.*

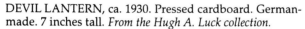

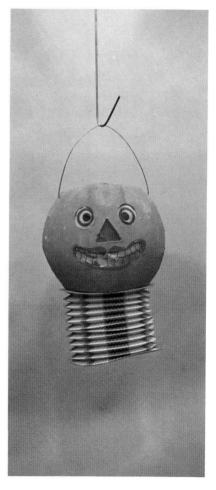

LANTERN, ca. 1930. Composition. German-made. 5 inches tall. *From the Hugh A. Luck collection.*

LANTERN, ca. 1925. Pressed and formed paperboard Jack-O'-Lantern with tissue paper inserts and accordion bottom. 8 inches tall, Made in Germany.

129

LANTERNS, ca. 1925-1935. A great collection of unusual German lanterns all of pressed paperboard. *From the Hugh A. Luck collection.*

LANTERN, ca. 1935. A paperboard devil's head lantern with tissue inserts. 7.5 inches tall.

LANTERN, ca. 1930. Pressed cardboard. German-made. 5 inches tall. *From the Hugh A. Luck collection.*

LANTERN, ca. 1930. A paperboard owl face lantern with tissue inserts. 15 inches wide by 8 inches tall.

LANTERN, ca. 1930. A paper lantern with tissue inserts. 12 inches tall.

LANTERN, ca. 1935. A painted tin owl lantern. 5.5 inches tall.

LANTERN, ca. 1935. A painted tin cat lantern. 5.5 inches tall.

LANTERN, ca. 1935. A papier mache cat with tissue paper inserts. 7 inches tall.

LANTERNS, ca. 1935. Papier mache Jack-O'-Lanterns that may have originally had tissue paper inserts. 4 & 7.5 inches tall.

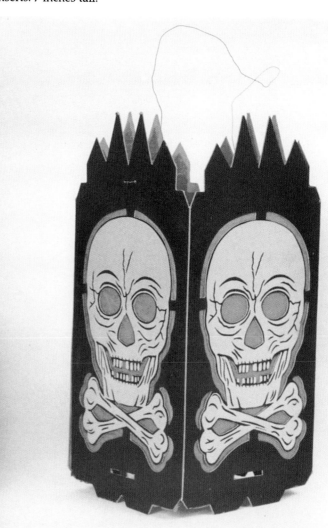

LANTERNS, ca. 1935. Two papier mache lanterns with tissue paper inserts, a Jack-O'-Lantern with a scary face, made in U.S.A. and a cat possibly German. Both 7 inches tall.

LANTERN, ca. 1935. Skull and cross bones of paperboard and thin paper. 10 inches tall. *From the Chris J. Russell and the Halloween Queen collection.*

LANTERNS, ca. 1938. Two papier mache lanterns with tissue paper inserts, a Jack-O'-Lantern with a scary face and a cat face made in U.S.A.. 6 & 5 inches tall.

LANTERN, ca. 1940. A papier mache cat with tissue paper inserts. 5.5 inches tall.

LANTERN, ca. 1940. Skulls and cats of paperboard and thin paper. Marked "Knorpp Candy Co., New York". 6.5 inches tall. *From the Chris J. Russell and the Halloween Queen collection.*

LANTERN, ca. 1940. Witch head of paperboard and thin paper. Has a happy face on one side and a sad face on the other. 6.5 inches tall. *From the Chris J. Russell and the Halloween Queen collection.*

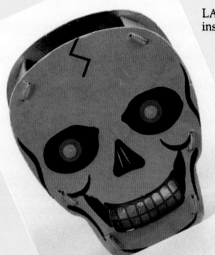

LANTERN, ca. 1940. A paperboard skull lantern with tissue inserts. 7.5 inches tall.

LANTERNS, ca. 1950. Glass and tin owls. Battery operated, 5 inches tall, made in Hong Kong or Japan. *From the Chris J. Russell and the Halloween Queen collection.*

LANTERN, ca. 1955. A papier mache Jack-O'-Lantern with tissue paper inserts. 6.5 inches tall.

LANTERNS, ETC., 1930-1960 A nice grouping of lanterns with a few candy containers thrown in for balance.

134

JACK-O'-LANTERN, ca. 1955. Fine grained pulp (papier mache) lantern with paper inserts. USA-made and 7.75 inches tall. *From the Hugh A. Luck collection.*

LANTERN, ca. 1958. A lithographed tin Jack-O'-Lantern. 5.5 inches tall. Made by U.S. Metal Toy Co.

LANTERNS, ca. 1960. Plastic and tin witch and devil. The plastic version is rarer than the glass version. Battery operated, 4.5 inches tall, made in Hong Kong.

LANTERN, ca. 1960. A glass and tin Jack-O'-Lantern. Battery operated, 6 inches tall, made in Hong Kong.

LANTERN, ca. 1960. Glass and tin skull. Battery operated, 5 inches tall, made in Hong Kong.

vegetable people, figurines and candy containers

PUMPKIN HEAD WITCH, 1905. A very early hand-painted glass candy container.

CANDY CONTAINERS, ca. 1905. A group of early glass candy containers, German-made, 4 inches tall. *From the Chris J. Russell and the Halloween Queen collection.*

CANDY CONTAINER, ca.1905. Great Jack-O'-Lantern bell, made in Germany. Opens at bottom. 3.75 inches tall. *From the Chris J. Russell and the Halloween Queen collection.*

CANDY CONTAINERS, ca.1915. Two great characters made of composition, German-made, 3.5 inches tall. The one on the left opens at the bottom and the one on the right opens at the neck. *From the Chris J. Russell and the Halloween Queen collection.*

PUMPKIN HEAD WITCH, ca.1908. A very early hand-painted glass candy container. 5 inches tall. *From the Chris J. Russell and the Halloween Queen collection.*

CANDY CONTAINERS, ca.1915. Two small (3.75 inches tall) composition candy containers that were made in Germany. They were hollow and filled with candy. A paper plug fit into the bottom hole to hold the candy in.

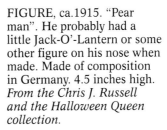

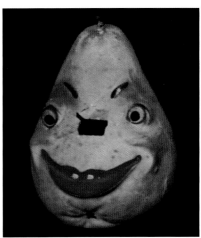

FIGURE, ca.1915. "Pear man". He probably had a little Jack-O'-Lantern or some other figure on his nose when made. Made of composition in Germany. 4.5 inches high. *From the Chris J. Russell and the Halloween Queen collection.*

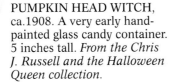

CANDY CONTAINER, ca.1915. Pumpkin boy on Jack-O'-Lantern, composition, made in Germany. Opens at bottom. 3.5 inches tall. *From the Chris J. Russell and the Halloween Queen collection.*

CANDY CONTAINER, ca. 1915. Winking pumpkin boy, composition, made in Germany. Opens at neck. 3.25 inches tall. *From the Chris J. Russell and the Halloween Queen collection.*

CANDY CONTAINER, 2003. A group of talented craftsmen are making modern-day candy containers and other sculptural pieces in the style of the early Halloween pieces. These are not Chinese knock-offs, but original art that often sells for hundreds of dollars. This piece is called "Batty" and stands 4.5 inches tall. It was made by Michael Bonfiglis.

MECHANICAL FIGURE, ca. 1916. The pumpkin man beats the drum and gets taller when the handle is turned. German-made, 6.25 inches tall. *From the Chris J. Russell and the Halloween Queen collection.*

MECHANICAL CANDY CONTAINER, ca. 1915. This is one of the best candy containers that you will ever see. A small wire handle near the witch's hand turns and a black cat comes out of the hole and into the witch's mouth. The witch is composition and the box is paper-covered wood, German-made, 6 inches tall. *From the Chris J. Russell and the Halloween Queen collection.*

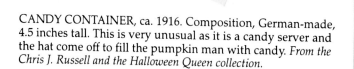

CANDY CONTAINER, ca. 1916. Composition, German-made, 4.5 inches tall. This is very unusual as it is a candy server and the hat come off to fill the pumpkin man with candy. *From the Chris J. Russell and the Halloween Queen collection.*

MECHANICAL FIGURE, ca. 1916. The pumpkin man sticks his tongue out when squeezed. German-made, 7 inches tall. *From the Chris J. Russell and the Halloween Queen collection.*

CANDY CONTAINER, ca. 1916. "The Drunken Goblin". A great, early, composition candy container, German-made, 6.5 inches tall. This is an example of an exceptional candy container. It is complex, humorous, whimsical and is in nice condition. *From the Chris J. Russell and the Halloween Queen collection.*

FIGURES, ca. 1916. Halloween paperboard figures, German-made, 3 inches tall. These probably would have been used as table decorations or possibly a bowl them over type of game. *From the Chris J. Russell and the Halloween Queen collection.*

CANDY CONTAINER, ca. 1916. Devil in composition, German-made, 5.5 inches tall. *From the Chris J. Russell and the Halloween Queen collection.*

CANDY CONTAINERS, ca. 1916. Pumpkin men, composition, German-made, 6 inches and 5.25 inches tall. *From the Chris J. Russell and the Halloween Queen collection.*

CANDY CONTAINERS, ca. 1916. "Squash Foot Jack-O'-Lantern Man" and "Goblin With a Basket", composition, German-made, 4.25 inches and 5.25 inches tall. The Squash Foot guy is exceptionally whimsical. He even has a little Jack-O'-Lantern on a spring for a nose. *From the Chris J. Russell and the Halloween Queen collection.*

CANDY CONTAINERS, ca. 1916. An incredible array of five luggage-shaped containers made of paper-covered pressed board, made in Germany. The orange one is worth 25% of the others. Average height is 2 inches tall. *From the Chris J. Russell and the Halloween Queen collection.*

CANDY CONTAINER, ca. 1916. A great, early, dashing pumpkin man composition candy container, German-made, 6.5 inches tall. *From the Chris J. Russell and the Halloween Queen collection.*

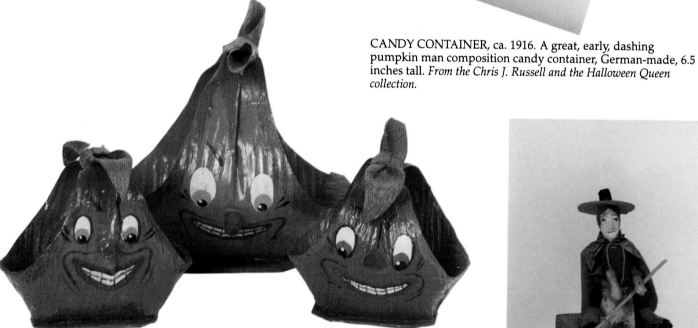

CANDY CONTAINERS, ca. 1916. Paperboard candy basket containers, German-made, 3.5 inches to 5 inches tall. *From the Chris J. Russell and the Halloween Queen collection.*

CANDY CONTAINER, ca. 1918. "Witch and Broom", crepe-covered paperboard with composition face. 4.75 inches tall. *From the Chris J. Russell and the Halloween Queen collection.*

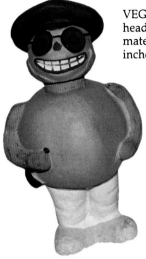

VEGETABLE FIGURE, ca. 1920. A pumpkin man figure, the head was removable and the body may have held candy. The material is composition and the piece was made in Germany. 8 inches tall.

VEGETABLE FIGURE, ca. 1920. A pumpkin man on a chicken, the head is removable and the body holds candy. The material is composition and the piece was made in Germany. 6 inches tall.

CANDY CONTAINER, 2003. This piece is called "Veggie Man" and stands 8.0 inches tall. It was made by Michael Bonfiglis.

CAT FIGURE, ca. 1920. A cat lady with removable head. The head is composition and the body was cardboard. Made in Germany. 11 inches tall.

NODDER, ca. 1920. A pumpkin head figure. The material is composition and the piece most likely was made in German. 7 inches tall.

VEGETABLE FIGURE, ca. 1920. A very unusual pumpkin headed scarecrow figure with a fly buzzing about his head. Years ago, the head may have been removable and the body may have held candy. The material is composition and the piece most likely was made in Germany. 5 inches tall.

WITCH FIGURE, ca. 1920. A pumpkin head witch, the head is removable and the body held candy. The material is composition and the piece was made in Germany. 7 inches tall.

CANDY CONTAINER, ca. 1920. "Pumpkin Head Witch" crepe-covered wire and paperboard, opens at base, 5.5 inches tall. *From the Chris J. Russell and the Halloween Queen collection.*

CANDY CONTAINER, ca. 1920. "Jack-O'-Lantern in Witch's Hat" composition and crepe-covered paperboard. German-made, opens at base, 3.75 inches tall. *From the Chris J. Russell and the Halloween Queen collection.*

CANDY CONTAINER, ca. 1920. Black cat box, paperboard, German-made, 2.5 inches tall. *From the Chris J. Russell and the Halloween Queen collection.*

CANDY CONTAINER, ca. 1920. "Cat on Jack-O'-Lantern" composition, German-made, opens at base, 3.75 inches tall. *From the Chris J. Russell and the Halloween Queen collection.*

CANDY CONTAINER, 2003. This piece is called "HeeBeeGeeBees" and it stands 12 inches tall. It was made by Debbie Hawkins.

CANDY CONTAINER, ca. 1920. Composition, German-made, opens at base, 4 inches tall. *From the Chris J. Russell and the Halloween Queen collection.*

CANDY CONTAINERS, ca. 1920. Old lady and pumpkin witch composition containers made in Germany. 4 inches and 5.5 inches tall. *From the Chris J. Russell and the Halloween Queen collection.*

CANDY CONTAINER, ca. 1920. "Oops, I ate too much candy" composition container made in Germany. Opens at the neck. 5.25 inches tall. *From the Chris J. Russell and the Halloween Queen collection.*

HALLOWEEN FIGURES, ca. 1920. A group of German composition figures listed left to right and top to bottom: 6 inch cat holding pumpkin with bottom plug; 5 inch pumpkin man with removable head; 7 inch cat on skull with bottom plug; 7 inch pumpkin man clown with removable head; 3 inch cat on candy box base; 3.5 inch devil on candy box base; 6 inch pumpkin man lantern holding lantern; 3.5 inch ghost on candy box base.

CANDY CONTAINER, ca. 1920. Black composition cat on a box container, made in Germany. Opens at the bottom. 2 inches tall. *From the Chris J. Russell and the Halloween Queen collection.*

CANDY CONTAINER, ca. 1920. "Automobile Driver in a Dust Jacket" composition container, made in Germany. Opens at the neck. 5 inches tall. *From the Chris J. Russell and the Halloween Queen collection.*

CANDY CONTAINER, ca. 1920.
Pumpkin man composition container,
made in Germany. Opens at the neck.
4.5 inches tall. *From the Chris J. Russell
and the Halloween Queen collection.*

CANDY CONTAINER & FIGURE,
ca. 1920. "Vegetable Farmer" and kid
goblin figure, composition, made in
Germany. 4.25 inches and 2 inches
tall. *From the Chris J. Russell and the
Halloween Queen collection.*

CANDY CONTAINERS, ca. 1920.
"Street Light and Jack-O'-Lantern
squeeker", crepe-covered paperboard
with composition cat. 4.5 inches and
4 inches tall. *From the Chris J. Russell
and the Halloween Queen collection.*

CANDY CONTAINER, ca. 1920.
"Jack-O'-Lantern head with broom",
crepe-covered paperboard with
pressed paperboard head. German-
made. 4.75 inches tall. *From the Chris
J. Russell and the Halloween Queen
collection.*

CANDY CONTAINER, ca. 1920.
"Buck Teeth - One Shoe On, One
Shoe Off", composition, German-
made, opens at neck. She has crossed
glass eyes. Glass eyes give her extra
value. 6 inches tall. *From the Chris J.
Russell and the Halloween Queen
collection.*

CANDY CONTAINER, ca. 1920.
"Jack-O'-Lantern Head Brownie",
composition, German-made, opens at
neck. 5.5 inches tall. *From the Chris J.
Russell and the Halloween Queen
collection.*

CANDY CONTAINER, ca. 1920. Crepe-covered paperboard, 3.75 inches tall. *From the Chris J. Russell and the Halloween Queen collection.*

CANDY CONTAINER, ca. 1920. "Policeman Cat", composition, German-made, 6 inches tall. *From the Chris J. Russell and the Halloween Queen collection.*

CANDY CONTAINER, ca. 1920. "Squeeker Bird", Pressed paperboard, German-made, opens at body with squeeker base. 7 inches tall. *From the Chris J. Russell and the Halloween Queen collection.*

FIGURE, ca. 1920. "Squeeker Witch". Head and feet are composition, made in Germany. 5 inches high. *From the Chris J. Russell and the Halloween Queen collection.*

CANDY HOLDER, ca. 1920. "Wide Mouth Jack-O'-Lantern". Made in Germany, pressed paperboard. 2.5 inches high. *From the Chris J. Russell and the Halloween Queen collection.*

CANDY CONTAINERS, ca. 1920. "Kid on Jack-O'-Lantern", composition, German-made, opens at bottom, 2.5 inches tall. *From the Chris J. Russell and the Halloween Queen collection.*

CANDY HOLDER, ca. 1920. "Wide Mouth Jack-O'-Lantern with Top Hat". Made in Germany, pressed paperboard. 4.5 inches high. *From the Chris J. Russell and the Halloween Queen collection.*

CANDY CONTAINER, ca. 1920. "Parade Leader", composition, German-made, opens at neck, 3.75 inches tall. *From the Chris J. Russell and the Halloween Queen collection.*

CANDY CONTAINERS, ca. 1920. Composition, German-made, open at bottom, 3.5 inches tall. *From the Chris J. Russell and the Halloween Queen collection.*

FIGURES, ca. 1920. Composition made in Germany. 3.5 inches high. *From the Chris J. Russell and the Halloween Queen collection.*

CANDY CONTAINER, ca. 1920. Composition, German-made, opens at neck, 3.5 inches tall. *From the Chris J. Russell and the Halloween Queen collection.*

CANDY CONTAINER, ca. 1920. Composition, German-made, opens at bottom, 3.5 inches tall. *From the Chris J. Russell and the Halloween Queen collection.*

FIGURE, ca. 1920. Composition made in Germany. 3.25 inches high. *From the Chris J. Russell and the Halloween Queen collection.*

FIGURE, ca. 1920. "Auto Driver". Composition, German-made, 2.25 inches tall. *From the Chris J. Russell and the Halloween Queen collection.*

CANDY CONTAINERS, ca. 1920. "The Old Sailor" and "The Goblin", composition, German-made, open at neck, 4.5 inches tall. *From the Chris J. Russell and the Halloween Queen collection.*

CANDY CONTAINER, ca. 1920. "The Pirate", composition, German-made, opens at neck, 4.5 inches tall. *From the Chris J. Russell and the Halloween Queen collection.*

CANDY CONTAINER, ca. 1920. "Hands in Pockets", composition, German-made, opens at neck, 4.75 inches tall. *From the Chris J. Russell and the Halloween Queen collection.*

CANDY CONTAINERS, ca. 1920. Composition, German-made, open at neck, 3.5 inches and 4.75 inches tall. *From the Chris J. Russell and the Halloween Queen collection.*

FIGURE, ca. 1920. Composition, German-made, 2.25 inches tall. *From the Chris J. Russell and the Halloween Queen collection.*

CANDY CONTAINER, ca. 1920. "Admiral Pumpkin". A composition candy container, German-made, 5 inches tall. *From the Chris J. Russell and the Halloween Queen collection.*

CANDY CONTAINERS, ca. 1920. Composition, German-made, open at base, 3 inches tall. *From the Chris J. Russell and the Halloween Queen collection.*

CANDY CONTAINER, ca. 1920. Composition and paperboard, German-made, 3 inches tall. *From the Chris J. Russell and the Halloween Queen collection.*

NODDER, ca. 1920. A cigar smoking man composition nodder, German-made, 5.5 inches tall. *From the Chris J. Russell and the Halloween Queen collection.*

CANDY CONTAINER, ca. 1920. A great, large, Jack-O'-Lantern composition candy container, German-made, 7.5 inches tall. This would have held an entire box of candy. *From*

CANDY CONTAINER, ca. 1920. Hollow paperboard candy container, German-made, 6 inches tall. *From the Chris J. Russell and the Halloween Queen collection.*

CANDY CONTAINERS, ca. 1920. A hollow pressed paper-board Jack-O'-Lantern on a stick and a composition pumpkin man candy container, German-made, 5 inches and 6.5 inches tall. *From the Chris J. Russell and the Halloween Queen collection.*

CANDY CONTAINERS, ca. 1920. Devils, composition, German-made, 6 inches tall. *From the Chris J. Russell and the Halloween Queen collection.*

CANDY CONTAINERS, ca. 1920. The one on the left is made of composition-covered pressed paperboard and opens at the bottom. The one on the right is all composition and opens at the bottom. 4.5 inches and 4 inches tall. German. *From the Chris J. Russell and the Halloween Queen collection.*

CANDY CONTAINER, ca. 1920. Owl, composition, German-made, 3.75 inches tall. The head may seem to be a replacement, but there are several known examples with the pumpkin head. German. *From the Chris J. Russell and the Halloween Queen collection.*

CANDY CONTAINERS, ca. 1920. Dutch boy and girl, made of composition and open at the neck. 3 inches tall. German. *From the Chris J. Russell and the Halloween Queen collection.*

CANDY CONTAINER, ca. 1920. "Pumpkin Head Cat" composition, German-made, opens at neck, 5.5 inches long. *From the Chris J. Russell and the Halloween Queen collection.*

CANDY CONTAINERS, ca. 1920. Two great cat, composition candy containers, German-made, 3 inches and 4 inches tall. *From the Chris J. Russell and the Halloween Queen collection.*

NODDER, ca. 1920. A tyrolian hatted man composition nodder, German-made, 6.5 inches tall. *From the Chris J. Russell and the Halloween Queen collection.*

FIGURES, ca. 1920. Two nice cat, composition figures, German-made, 4.5 inches and 3 inches tall. *From the Chris J. Russell and the Halloween Queen collection.*

MECHANICAL FIGURE, ca. 1920. The pumpkin man moves his arms and legs and dances when squeezed. German-made, 6.5 inches tall. *From the Chris J. Russell and the Halloween Queen collection.*

NODDER, ca. 1920. Cigar smoker made of composition, German, 4.75 inches tall. *From the Chris J. Russell and the Halloween Queen collection.*

FIGURE, ca. 1920. Large pumpkin man roly poly, Schoenhut figure, German-made, 8.5 inches tall. A scarce Schoenhut piece that is worth more because Schoenhut collectors want it, too. *From the Chris J. Russell and the Halloween Queen collection.*

CANDY CONTAINER, ca. 1920. A large, wonderful cat on a turnip, composition candy container, opens at bottom, German-made, 6 inches across. *From the Chris J. Russell and the Halloween Queen collection.*

CANDY CONTAINERS, ca. 1920. Crepe-covered paperboard, 3.75 inches tall. *From the Chris J. Russell and the Halloween Queen collection.*

CANDY CONTAINER, ca. 1920. "Jack-O'-Lantern with a Hat" paperboard, double faced - one side smiles and the other frowns - German-made, opens at base, 4.75 inches tall. *From the Chris J. Russell and the Halloween Queen collection.*

FIGURE, ca. 1920. This looks to be a Dennison crepe piece created with a bisque doll, crepe paper and some small cat figures, 3.25 inches tall. *From the Chris J. Russell and the Halloween Queen collection.*

CANDY CONTAINER, ca. 1920. A large, great goblin with a smile, composition candy container, German-made, 6.5 inches tall. *From the Chris J. Russell and the Halloween Queen collection.*

CANDY CONTAINERS, ca. 1920. Composition candy containers, German-made, 2.5 inches to 3.5 inches tall. *From the Chris J. Russell and the Halloween Queen collection.*

FIGURES, ca. 1920. A family of Halloween characters, composition or plaster, German-made, 2 inches tall all seen over by a 4.5 inch cigarette smoking father figure of composition and hollow paperboard. *From the Chris J. Russell and the Halloween Queen collection.*

NODDER, ca. 1920. A smiling girl composition nodder, German-made, 6 inches tall. *From the Chris J. Russell and the Halloween Queen collection.*

FIGURES, ca. 1920. Composition, German-made top hatted pumpkin man, 3.25 inches tall and a hollow plaster witch, 3 inches tall. *From the Chris J. Russell and the Halloween*

CANDY CONTAINER, ca. 1920. "Jack-O'-Lantern Streetlight" crepe-covered paperboard, German-made, opens at base, 4 inches tall. *From the Chris J. Russell and the Halloween Queen collection.*

TALL WITCH, ca. 1920. This smiling witch candy container is dressed in muslin cloth and is made of composition. It is German-made and opens from the middle. There is a "Huylers Candies" label on the pull slide. 11 inches tall. *From the Hugh A. Luck collection.*

MECHANICAL WITCH, ca. 1920. This German-made witch holds a candy bowl and is dressed in linen and felt. The head is composition. It winds up and walks. 10 inches tall. *From the Hugh A. Luck collection.*

CANDY CONTAINER, ca. 1920. "Witch's House" crepe-covered paperboard, German-made, opens at base, 5 inches tall. *From the Chris J. Russell and the Halloween Queen collection.*

CANDY CONTAINERS, ca. 1920. Devils, composition, German-made, 3 inches tall. *From the Chris J. Russell and the Halloween Queen collection.*

CANDY CONTAINERS, ca. 1920. Cats, composition, German-made, open at base, 2 to 4.25 inches tall. *From the Chris J. Russell and the Halloween Queen collection.*

JACK-O'-LANTERN HEADED FIGURE, ca. 1920. Composition candy container - a veggie man with glasses. It is German-made and opens at the neck. 5 inches tall. *From the Hugh A. Luck collection.*

CANDY CONTAINERS, ca. 1920. Goblin and skeleton, composition, German-made, 4 inches tall. *From the Chris J. Russell and the Halloween Queen collection.*

CANDY CONTAINERS, ca. 1920. Goblins, composition, German-made, 3.5 to 4 inches tall. *From the Chris J. Russell and the Halloween Queen collection.*

FIGURES, ca. 1920. Goblins is composition and the Jack-O'-Lantern is hollow painted paperboard, German-made, 4 inches tall. *From the Chris J. Russell and the Halloween Queen collection.*

JACK-O'-LANTERN HEADED BELLHOP FIGURE, ca. 1920. Composition candy container. It is German-made and opens at the neck. 7 inches tall.

CARROT-SHAPED CANDY CON-TAINER, ca. 1920. Papier mache candy container, German-made and opens at the base. 6 inches tall. *From the Hugh A. Luck collection.*

JACK-O'-LANTERN WITCH HEADED FIGURE, ca. 1920. Composition candy container. It is German-made and opens at the neck. 6 inches tall. *From the Hugh A. Luck collection.*

WHISTLE FIGURE, ca. 1920. Papier mache candy container, German-made and opens at the base. 7.5 inches tall. *From the Hugh A. Luck collection.*

GOBLIN FIGURE WITH CAT, ca. 1920. Composition candy container. German-made and opens at the bottom. 6 inches tall *From the Hugh A. Luck collection.*

GOBLIN FIGURE, ca. 1920. Composition candy container. It is German-made and opens at the bottom. 9 inches tall. *From the Hugh A. Luck collection.*

JACK-O'-LANTERN HEADED FIGURE, ca. 1920. Composition candy container. It is German-made and opens at the neck. 5.5 inches tall. *From the Hugh A. Luck collection.*

DEVIL FIGURE, ca. 1920. Composition candy container. German-made and opens at the neck. 5.5 inches tall. *From the Hugh A. Luck collection.*

FIGURES, ca. 1920. Composition Halloween figures. The cat on the pumpkin is a candy container. German-made. 4 - 4.5 inches tall. *From the Hugh A. Luck collection.*

TALL GOBLIN, ca. 1920. A pressed cardboard candy container in Halloween colors. It is German-made and opens in the middle. 9.5 inches tall. *From the Hugh A. Luck collection.*

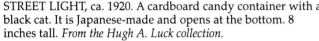

STREET LIGHT, ca. 1920. A cardboard candy container with a black cat. It is Japanese-made and opens at the bottom. 8 inches tall. *From the Hugh A. Luck collection.*

CANDY CONTAINERS, ca. 1920. Two composition candy containers in miscellaneous shapes and a Jack-O'-Lantern man on bird figure. German-made. 4.5 inches to 5.5 inches tall. *From the Hugh A. Luck collection.*

SMILING GHOST, ca. 1920. A composition nodder candy container. Made in Germany and opens at the bottom. Ghosts, while traditional Halloween figures, rarely show up as candy containers. 6 inches tall. *From the Hugh A. Luck collection.*

BOY WITH PARADE LANTERN, ca. 1920. A composition figure that is German-made. 2.5 inches tall. *From the Hugh A. Luck collection.*

WITCH IN PUMPKIN, ca. 1920. Composition candy container. It is German-made and opens at the bottom. 5.5 inches tall. *From the Hugh A. Luck collection.*

SPRING ARM WITCH, ca. 1920. A composition figure with a bright red face. It is German-made and 7 inches tall. *From the Hugh A. Luck collection.*

PUPPET, ca. 1920. Pressed cardboard puppet with wooden hands & feet. German-made and 6.25 inches tall in sitting position. *From the Hugh A. Luck collection.*

CANDY CONTAINERS, ca. 1920. Composition, German-made, 3.5 inches and 2.5 inches tall. *From the Chris J. Russell and the Halloween Queen collection.*

CANDY CONTAINERS, ca. 1920. Pressed and formed paper-board candy holders in unusual shapes, 5 inches and 5.5 inches tall. German-made. *From the Chris J. Russell and the Halloween Queen collection.*

CANDY CONTAINER, ca. 1920. "The Chef", composition, made in Germany. Opens at neck. 4.75 inches tall. *From the Chris J. Russell and the Halloween Queen collection.*

CANDY CONTAINER, ca. 1920. Tin litho, American made candy box with a fortune telling device, 5.5 inches tall. *From the Chris J. Russell and the Halloween Queen collection.*

FIGURE, ca. 1920. "Squash Body Bird man", composition, German-made, 7.5 inches tall. *From the Chris J. Russell and the Halloween Queen collection.*

BABY FACE VEGGIE MAN, ca. 1920. Composition candy container with a lantern head. It opens at the neck. 7 inches tall, German. *From the Hugh A. Luck collection.*

CANDY CONTAINERS, ca. 1920. "The Maitre D' and helper", composition, made in Germany. Both open at neck. 4.75 inches and 3.75 inches tall. *From the Chris J. Russell and the Halloween Queen collection.*

CAT ON JACK-O'-LANTERN, ca. 1920. Composition candy container. It is German-made and opens from the bottom. 6 inches tall. *From the Hugh A. Luck collection.*

CANDY CONTAINER, ca. 1920. A striking composition devil's head candy container that opens from the bottom. 6 inches tall. *From the Hugh A. Luck collection.*

GOBLIN ON A LOG, ca. 1920. Composition candy container of a George Washington type figure (wig, ponytail & hatchet), German-made and opens at the neck. 5 inches tall. *From the Hugh A. Luck collection.*

CANDY HOLDERS, ca. 1925. Painted bisque figures, made in Germany. 3.5 inches tall. *From the Chris J. Russell and the Halloween Queen collection.*

CANDY HOLDERS, ca. 1925. Painted bisque figures, made in Germany. 3 inches tall. *From the Chris J. Russell and the Halloween Queen collection.*

CANDY BOX, ca. 1925. 3 inches tall. Paper-covered cardboard. The illustrations are probably by Grace Drayton. *From the Chris J. Russell and the Halloween Queen collection.*

CANDY HOLDERS, ca. 1925. Probably made to hold lollipops. Painted bisque figures, made in Germany. 5 inches tall. *From the Chris J. Russell and the Halloween Queen collection.*

CANDY CONTAINER, ca. 1925. Pumpkin man with a cigar, pressed paper and composition, made in Germany. The head opens to hold the candy and the neck is a spring. 4.5 inches tall. *From the Chris J. Russell and the Halloween Queen collection.*

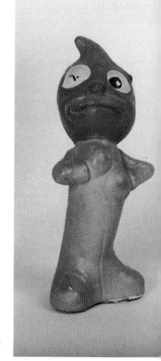

CANDY CONTAINERS, ca. 1925. "Goblin In a Cat's Mouth" and "Googly Eye Cat", composition, German-made, 6.5 inches and 6 inches tall. *From the Chris J. Russell and the Halloween Queen collection.*

FIGURE, ca. 1925. Standoff goblin, composition or plaster figure, German-made, 6 inches tall. *From the Chris J. Russell and the Halloween Queen collection.*

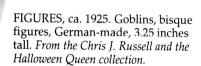

FIGURES, ca. 1925. Goblins, bisque figures, German-made, 3.25 inches tall. *From the Chris J. Russell and the Halloween Queen collection.*

CANDY CONTAINER, ca. 1925. "Thornes Toffee" lithographed tin container, English made, 6.5 inches tall. *From the Chris J. Russell and the Halloween Queen collection.*

FIGURES, ca. 1925. Goblins, composition or plaster figures, German-made, 2.75 inches tall. *From the Chris J. Russell and the Halloween Queen collection.*

FIGURES, ca. 1925. Goblins with candy container hollow paperboard heads and felt bodies over wire, German-made, 11 inches tall. *From the Chris J. Russell and the Halloween Queen collection.*

PUMPKIN HEADED TRAIN, ca. 1925. Composition candy container. It is German-made and opens at the front. 5 inches tall.

FIGURES, ca. 1925. Halloween musical characters, composition German-made, 4 inches tall. *From the Chris J. Russell and the Halloween Queen collection.*

CANDY CONTAINER, ca. 1925. A large devil composition candy container, German-made, 7 inches tall. *From the Chris J. Russell and the Halloween Queen collection.*

FIGURE, ca. 1925. Kewpie doll and Jack-O'-Lantern, made in Germany. The Kewpie doll was created by Rose O'Neil. Many figures were made by her authorized company and by others stealing the image. Few were made for Halloween and this is a rare item. This has the Rose O'Neil Kewpie sticker on the back. 2 inches tall. *From the Chris J. Russell and the Halloween Queen collection.*

CANDY CONTAINER, ca. 1925. Crepe-covered paperboard with composition face, 5 inches tall. *From the Chris J. Russell and the Halloween Queen collection.*

FIGURES, ca. 1925. Halloween characters, composition or plaster, German-made, 5.25 inches and 4 inches tall. *From the Chris J. Russell and the Halloween Queen collection.*

CANDY HOLDERS, ca. 1925. Painted bisque figures, made in Germany. 3.75 inches tall. *From the Chris J. Russell and the Halloween Queen collection.*

CANDY BOX, ca. 1925. Crepe-covered stuffing in the shape of a pumpkin covered a box of fine chocolates suitable for the suitor. 6.5 inches wide by 3.5 inches high.

CANDY CONTAINER, ca. 1928. "Cat on the Hat" composition and paperboard, German-made, opens at base, 3.5 inches tall. *From the Chris J. Russell and the Halloween Queen collection.*

SCULPTURE, 2003. This piece is called "Boogie Goodie Bag" and it stands 9 inches tall. It was made by Rucus Studios.

FIGURE, ca. 1930. Celluloid musician with a bell inside. Made in Germany. 4.5 inches. *From the Chris J. Russell and the Halloween Queen collection.*

FIGURES, ca. 1930. Celluloid owls. Made in Germany. 5.5 inches high. *From the Chris J. Russell and the Halloween Queen collection.*

FIGURE, ca. 1930. Celluloid roly poly. Made in Germany. 3 inches high. *From the Chris J. Russell and the Halloween Queen collection.*

CELLULOID FIGURES, ca. 1930. These thin blown celluloid figures were made in Japan. They may have been available into the 1950s, but do appear in early catalogs. They are hard to find and are very desirable. 3.25 inches tall. *From the Hugh A. Luck collection.*

CANDY CONTAINER, ca. 1930. A large devil hollow paper-board candy container, German-made, 7 inches tall. *From the Chris J. Russell and the Halloween Queen collection.*

TABLE DECORATIONS, ca. 1930. These little 2.5 inches tall candle men may have been candy containers. A bit of missing paper shows that the candles are composed of Japanese newspaper.

CAT SQUEEKER, ca. 1930. A cardboard candy container. It is German-made and opens at the bottom. 10 inches tall. *From the Hugh A. Luck collection.*

CAT & DEVIL FIGURES, ca. 1930. Hand-painted pressed board candy containers. German or Japanese, they open in the middle. 3.25 inches tall. *From the Hugh A. Luck collection.*

OWL FIGURE, ca. 1930. An owl with glass eyes. The material is papier mache and gesso. The bottom of the log removes to hold the candy. 6 inches tall.

FIGURES, ca. 1930. Celluloid roly polys. Made in Germany. 4 inches high. *From the Chris J. Russell and the Halloween Queen collection.*

FIGURES, ca. 1930. Celluloid roly polys. Made in Germany. 4 inches high. *From the Chris J. Russell and the Halloween Queen collection.*

FIGURES, ca. 1930. Celluloid witch with wagon and witch in race car. Made in Germany. 4 inches long. *From the Chris J. Russell and the Halloween Queen collection.*

FIGURES, ca. 1930. Celluloid witches with wagon. Made in Germany. 4 inches long. *From the Chris J. Russell and the Halloween Queen collection.*

FIGURES, ca. 1930. Celluloid owl and scarecrow. Made in Germany. 3.5 inches. *From the Chris J. Russell and the Halloween Queen collection.*

FIGURES, ca. 1930. Celluloid boys. Made in Germany. 4 inches and 3.5 inches. *From the Chris J. Russell and the Halloween Queen collection.*

FIGURE, ca. 1930. Celluloid clown. Made in Germany. 6 inches. *From the Chris J. Russell and the Halloween Queen collection.*

SKELETONS, ca. ?. These incredible pieces may be from the 1930s or may be much more recent. Japanese-made. Composition and wood and 3.5 inches tall. *From the Hugh A. Luck collection.*

CANDY JAR, ca. 1930. Fired pottery Jack-O'-Lantern, 4.5 inches tall. *From the Chris J. Russell and the Halloween Queen collection.*

FIGURES, ca. 1935. Bisque devil made in Japan, 3 inches tall and a plaster witch, 3.75 inches tall. *From the Chris J. Russell and the Halloween Queen collection.*

FIGURE, ca. 1935. Bisque Jack-O'-Lantern girl with cat made in Germany, 5.5 inches tall. *From the Chris J. Russell and the Halloween Queen collection.*

FIGURE, ca. 1935. Bisque witch made in Germany, 5.75 inches tall. *From the Chris J. Russell and the Halloween Queen collection.*

CANDY HOLDER, ca. 1935. Bisque lollipop holder made in Germany, 3 inches tall. *From the Chris J. Russell and the Halloween Queen collection.*

CANDY BOX, ca. 1935. "Owl", paperboard, 4 inches across. *From the Chris J. Russell and the Halloween Queen collection.*

CANDY HOLDER, ca. 1935. "Witch on Broomstick with Cauldron", painted metal, 3.5 inches tall. *From the Chris J. Russell and the Halloween Queen collection.*

FIGURES, 1930-1950. A grouping of chenille, composition, hard plastic and felt-covered wire figures from the U.S., Japan, and Germany.

CANDY CONTAINER, ca. 1940. "Witch with Cauldron" paperboard, made by Merri Lee, 3.75 inches tall. *From the Chris J. Russell and the Halloween Queen collection.*

WITCH FIGURE, ca. 1935. A pumpkin head witch, the head removes and the body held candy. The head is papier mache, the body is cardboard and crepe and the piece was made in Japan. 4.5 inches tall.

CANDY CONTAINER, ca. 1940. "Skeleton Pulling Wagon" cardboard, made in USA, 5 inches long. *From the Chris J. Russell and the Halloween Queen collection.*

CANDY HOLDER, ca. 1940. Pumpkin head man pulling a Sack, paperboard. 6.5 inches tall. *From the Chris J. Russell and the Halloween Queen collection.*

CANDY HOLDERS, ca. 1950. Tiny Jack-O'-Lanterns, 2.5 inches tall, made of papier mache held candy for the child's party.

CANDY CONTAINER, ca. 1945. Papier mache. Made by Master Craft in Newark, New Jersey. 3 inches tall. *From the Chris J. Russell and the Halloween Queen collection.*

WITCH, ca. 1955. Hard plastic candy container in Halloween colors made in the USA. 5.5 inches tall. *From the Hugh A. Luck collection.*

CANDY HOLDERS, ca. 1950. Hard plastic stand-up lollipop holders made in the USA. 4.5 inches tall. Almost all of the hard plastic Halloween pieces seem to have been made or distributed by the Rosen Company located in Rhode Island. *From the Chris J. Russell and the Halloween Queen collection.*

CAT ROLLER, ca. 1955. Hard plastic candy container in Halloween colors made in the USA. 5 inches tall. *From the Hugh A. Luck collection.*

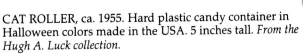

HARD PLASTIC FIGURES, ca. 1955. A nice grouping of unusual hard plastic candy containers and figurines in Halloween colors made in the USA. *From the Hugh A. Luck collection.*

CANDY CONTAINER, ca. 1991. Kewpie doll and Jack-O'-Lantern on a wooden box, made in Germany. 3 inches tall. *From the Chris J. Russell and the Halloween Queen collection.*

miscellaneous

SURPRISE BOX, ca. 1885. When you open the unassuming wooden box, a Jack-O'-Lantern man jumps up. His head is composition, cloth body, German-made and 12 inches tall extended. This is one of the earliest Halloween pieces we have seen. *From the Hugh A. Luck collection.*

JEWELRY, 1890. A 2.25 inch wide sterling silver moon and two owls with ruby eyes. This was probably made in England. It is unusual in that the owls are full three dimensional figures rather than the typical hollow backs usually found in jewelry.

DIE CUT CARD, 1888. "And swept the cobwebs from the sky" are the words on this great witch image. If this is a Halloween item, it is one of the earliest.

WINDOW, ca. 1895. A great stained glass image of an owl in a tree. *From the Chris J. Russell and the Halloween Queen collection.*

JEWELRY, 1890. This 2 inch wide sterling silver bat with a faceted, hollow back body was probably made in England. Most likely, they were not made for Halloween but would have been worn in the fall season.

BUTTONS, ca. 1904 & 1905. Halloween festival pins from Newark, New Jersey and Albany, New York. 2 inches in diameter and 1.75 inches in diameter. *From the Chris J. Russell and the Halloween Queen collection.*

JEWELRY, 1890. A 2.75 inch wide hollow back brass bat. The bat was a popular image in Victorian times.

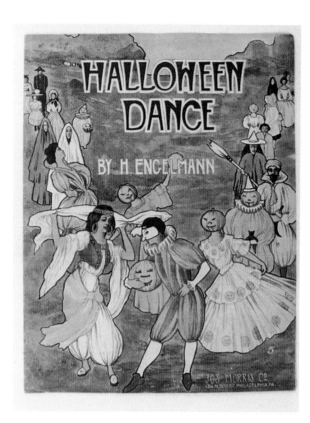

SHEET MUSIC, 1907. "Halloween Dance". Music with a Halloween theme. *From the Chris J. Russell and the Halloween Queen collection.*

YOUTH'S COMPANION, 1896. An early depiction of Halloween. *From the Chris J. Russell and the Halloween Queen collection.*

PHOTO, 1940s. This looks like the inside of a conservatory or botanical garden.

PROGRAM, 1905. Official program for the Halloween Carnival of Albany, New York. This was a society affair with a cast of hundreds. *From the Chris J. Russell and the Halloween Queen collection.*

SHEET MUSIC, 1908. "'Long in Pumpkin Pickin' Time". Music with a Halloween theme. *From the Chris J. Russell and the Halloween Queen collection.*

SHEET MUSIC, 1909. "Jack O'Lantern Boogieman". Music with a Halloween theme. *From the Chris J. Russell and the Halloween Queen collection.*

PHOTO, ca. 1910. A postcard real photo advertising calendar of a girl carving a Jack-O'-Lantern. *From the Chris J. Russell and the Halloween Queen collection.*

PAPER DOLL, ca. 1912. Caroline Chester's full base paper doll was from *Delineator Magazine*. *From the Chris J. Russell and the Halloween Queen collection.*

CARNIVAL CURRENCY, 1912 through 1933. Lewisburg, Ohio had a Halloween carnival each year and issued Halloween currency.

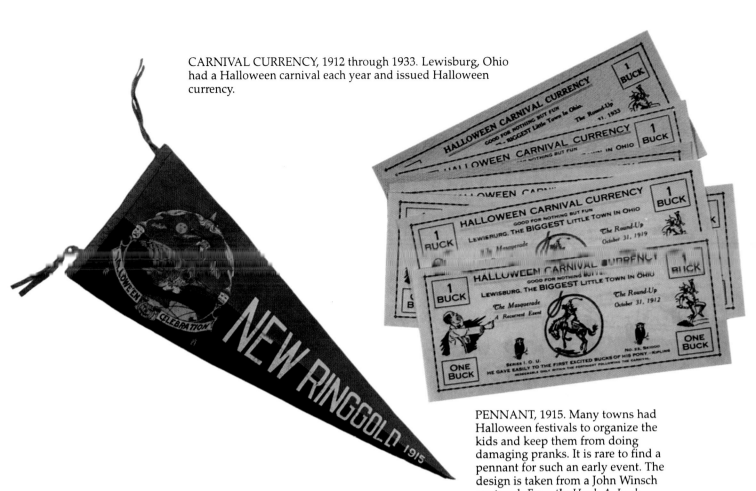

PENNANT, 1915. Many towns had Halloween festivals to organize the kids and keep them from doing damaging pranks. It is rare to find a pennant for such an early event. The design is taken from a John Winsch postcard. *From the Hugh A. Luck collection.*

PAPER DOLLS, 1917. A Halloween party for Betty Bonnet from the *Ladies Home Journal. From the Chris J. Russell and the Halloween Queen collection.*

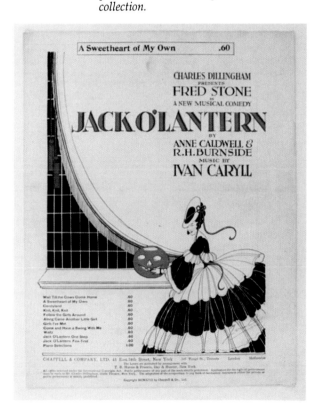

SHEET MUSIC, 1917. "Jack O'Lantern" was a musical play with a Halloween theme. This music was "A Sweetheart of My Own". *From the Chris J. Russell and the Halloween Queen collection.*

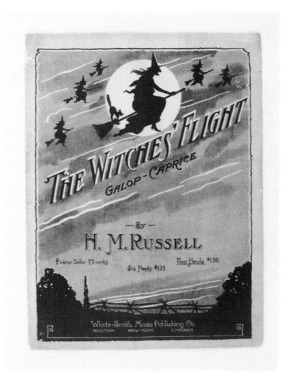

SHEET MUSIC, 1917. "The Witches' Flight". Music with a Halloween theme. This was originally published in 1875. *From the Chris J. Russell and the Halloween Queen collection.*

MAGAZINE, 1919. *Today's Housewife* has a great cover. *From Chris J. Russell and the Halloween Queen collection.*

BOX LABEL, ca. 1920. The box held 40 pounds of jelly beans and the product was made in Portland, Oregon. Note the reference to stopping the Halloween pranksters. "The Pranksters" was an 1890s skit about Halloween pranks - kids stealing gates and tipping over outhouses. An incredible image. *From the Chris J. Russell and the Halloween Queen collection.*

PAPER DOLLS, ca. 1920. "Polly Pratt Gives a Halloween Party". Note, no trick or treat bags yet. *From the Chris J. Russell and the Halloween Queen collection.*

PIN, ca. 1920. Articulated Jack-O'-Lantern man lapel pin is composition, made in Germany. 2.5 inches tall.

HOLSUM BREAD FOR HAL-LOWEEN, ca.1952. A nice advertising poster for Holsum Bread. It is about 36 inches tall.

STICKPINS, ca. 1920. Another nice group made from composition. Probably made in Germany. Each face is about 1 - 1.75 inches tall. *From the Chris J. Russell and the Halloween Queen collection.*

STICKPINS, ca. 1920. They are covered cork or wood, made in the USA. Each is about 1 inch tall. *From the Chris J. Russell and the Halloween Queen collection.*

PIN, ca. 1920. Jack-O'-Lantern man lapel pin is wood, made in Germany. 2 inches tall.

STICKPINS, ca. 1920. They are composition, made in Germany. Each face is about 1 inch tall. *From the Chris J. Russell and the Halloween Queen collection.*

2 PINS, ca. 1920. Jumping Jack lapel pin in the shape of a veggie man. Construction is lithographed paper on wood and painted wood, made in Germany. 2 inches tall.

FAN, ca. 1920. Printed paper and wood fan. A Halloween fan is a rare item. This is an exceptional piece since the artwork is designed for the fan as opposed to taking a standard image and using on a fan.

PINS, ca. 1920 & 1930. Googly eye Jack-O'-Lantern lapel pin is paper and composition and made in Germany. 1 inches tall. The jiggle eye tomato is papier mache and made in Japan. 1 inch tall.

PINS, ca. 1920. Devil lapel pin and the pumpkin fiddler are composition, made in Germany. 2 inches tall and 1.5 inches tall.

ADVERTISEMENT, ca. 1920. Diamond Brand Walnuts. *From the Chris J. Russell and the Halloween Queen collection.*

CANDLE HOLDERS, ca. 1920. "Devils". Made of metal. *From the Chris J. Russell and the Halloween Queen collection.*

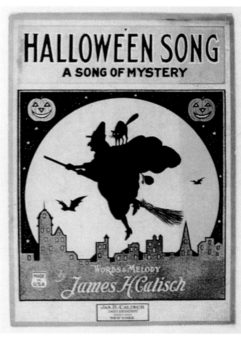

SHEET MUSIC, 1922. "Halloween Song". Music with a Halloween theme. *From the Chris J. Russell and the Halloween Queen collection.*

BOOKS, 1923 and 1935. Paine publishing *Spooky Halloween Entertainments* with recitations, monologues, readings, pantomimes, quotations, songs and ideas for Halloween parties designed for teachers at school. This was the time when organized Halloween celebration was being actively encouraged. *Hallowe'en*, by Robert H. Schauffler, is a similar type of book done in the 1930s.

TEA SET, ca. 1925. Tiny tea set (representative pieces shown), German-made, 1 to 3 inches tall. *From the Chris J. Russell and the Halloween Queen collection.*

MAGAZINE, 1922. The *Chicago Ledger* has a great image of a witch in a flying machine.

CANDY BOX DECORATION, ca. 1925. This 1.5 inch high painted raised tin Jack-O'-Lantern would have been added to the outside of a candy box.

FAN, ca. 1925. Printed paper and wood fan. 8.5 inches across. Made in Germany. *From the Chris J. Russell and the Halloween Queen collection.*

FAN, ca. 1925. Black cat on a fan. Thin paper and wood. 14 inches tall. Made in Germany. *From the Chris J. Russell and the Halloween Queen collection.*

BRIDGE MARKER, ca. 1928. This may be a homemade suit marker for the card game of bridge. After a suit or no trump is bid and the players must make their points according to their bid. 8 inches high. *From the Chris J. Russell and the Halloween Queen collection.*

BRACELET, ca. 1930. A Bakelite or early plastic bracelet with odd, pop-eyed Halloweenish figures. *From the Chris J. Russell and the Halloween Queen collection.*

MAGAZINE, 1928. *John Martin's Book - The Child's Magazine. From the Chris J. Russell and the Halloween Queen collection.*

ADVERTISEMENT, ca. 1929. Wrigley's Gum. *From the Chris J. Russell and the Halloween Queen collection.*

DOLL, ca. 1930. Felt material covers this Halloween doll. About 13 inches tall.

TROLLEY SIGN, ca. 1930. A great coffee ad with a Halloween theme. *From the Chris J. Russell and the Halloween Queen collection.*

TINY PITCHER, ca. 1935. Bisque, made by Thoelay Ware, England, 2 inches tall. *From the Chris J. Russell and the Halloween Queen collection.*

SIGN,1932. This sign may have hung during the days of Halloween tricksters and near the birth of Trick-or-Treating. *From the Chris J. Russell and the Halloween Queen collection.*

ASHTRAY, ca. 1935. Bisque, made in Japan, 4.5 inches tall. *From the Chris J. Russell and the Halloween Queen collection.*

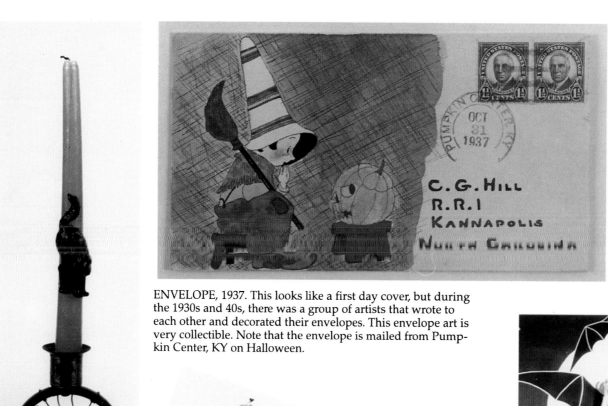

ENVELOPE, 1937. This looks like a first day cover, but during the 1930s and 40s, there was a group of artists that wrote to each other and decorated their envelopes. This envelope art is very collectible. Note that the envelope is mailed from Pumpkin Center, KY on Halloween.

PHOTO, ca. 1940. This Halloween lass was an actress named Nancy Carroll at Paramount Studios. Each studio would send out pictures of their actors and actresses in different poses to generate publicity. Often they had nothing to do with any particular movie. *From the Chris J. Russell and the Halloween Queen collection.*

CANDLE HOLDERS, ca. 1935. Craftsman-made copper candle holders with spiders on a spider web. About 8 inches tall without candles.

BOOT SCRAPER, ca. 1940. Cast iron witch-shaped boot scraper. This would go outside a door to clean the mud off shoes and boots before entering the house. I wonder what the reason was for making it in the shape of a witch. Was it good luck to rub your foot on the back of a witch?

PHOTO, 1908. Photo of a fraternity Halloween toga party.

MAGAZINE, 1942. *Child Life* has some great Halloween covers.

PHOTO, ca. 1946. Studio publicity photo. *From the Chris J. Russell and the Halloween Queen collection.*

PHOTO, ca. 1946. Universal Studio publicity photo. *From the Chris J. Russell and the Halloween Queen collection.*

ADVERTISEMENT, ca. 1948. Rheingold Beer stand-up ad. An entire collection can be made of Halloween theme ads. Someone should tell this lady that her candle is too tall. *From the Chris J. Russell and the Halloween Queen collection.*

BUTTON, ca. 1948-1955. Halloween Festival pins from Anaheim, California. The festival was begun in 1923. 1.75 inches in diameter and 2.25 inches in diameter.

FLASHLIGHTS, ca. 1948. Tiny Jack-O'-Lanterns light up when the sting was pulled. Made by E.J. Kahn & Co.

RAISINS FOR HALLOWEEN, ca.1957. This is a large (50 inches wide) in-store advertising poster suggesting that packs of raisins make great treats for trick or treaters. This is a beautiful piece that shows a group of kids in homemade and store-bought costumes that were popular in the late 1950s.

ADVERTISEMENT, ca. 1951. Old Gold Cigarettes. *From the Chris J. Russell and the Halloween Queen collection.*

SHEET MUSIC, 1951. Trick or Treat. Music with a Halloween theme. *From the Chris J. Russell and the Halloween Queen collection.*

JEWELRY, 1950. Witch head earrings 3.75 inches tall painted celluloid plastic.

JEWELRY, 1985. Cat earrings 3 inches tall painted wood.

PARTY BOOK, 1952. The Weenie Witch showed you all the things that you could do with hot-dogs to brighten up your Halloween party.

MAGAZINE, 1953. The children's magazines such as *Jack & Jill* give the collector some great covers and show the party ideas and costumes of the 1950s.

JEWELRY, 1955. A nice 1.75 inch tall plastic cat and Jack-O'-Lantern. Probably made in Japan.

COOKIE CUTTERS, ca. 1954. Six Halloween-shaped tin cutters. Maker unknown.

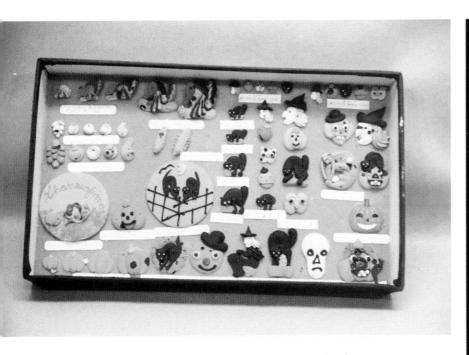

CAKE DECORATIONS, 1955. This is a salesman's sample of the decorations available. 14 inches by 22 inches.

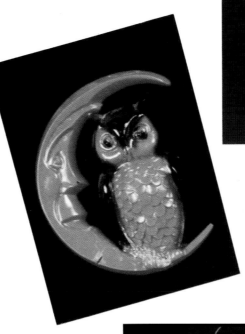

JEWELRY, ca. 1955. Skeleton pin made of plastic bones, spring for a neck and metal ring connectors. Probably made in Japan. 5 inches tall.

JEWELRY, 1955. Two variations of a 1.75 inch tall plastic owl in the moon. Probably made in Japan.

PLASTIC NOVELTIES, 1950-1990. This collection includes candy containers, party favors and push toys. For many years, few people collected the plastic items. But with the increase in price of some of the older items, these plastic treasures are rapidly being added to collections.

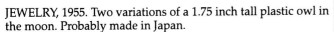

WITCHES, 1930-1960. A Halloween collection can be grouped according to subject matter. Here is the witch's corner.

DEVILS, 1920-1960. Devils appear much less threatening when assembled as a group.

CATS, 1930-1960. Another collection grouped according to subject matter. Here are the black cats.

BANK, ca. 1958. The Brumberger Haunted House Mystery Bank. Tin and plastic construction. Put a coin on the doorstep and ghostly figures appear and the coin vanishes. 8 inches high. *From the Chris J. Russell and the Halloween Queen collection.*

ART WORK, ca. 1967. Original artwork for a Halloween Card. 6 inches tall.

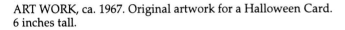

ART WORK, ca. 1960. Original artwork for a Halloween party book or decoration. Original Halloween artwork is very hard to find. 12 inches tall. *From the Hugh A. Luck collection.*

TOY, ca. 1963. The Marx Hootin' Hollow Haunted House. Tin and plastic construction. Push a key on the side of the house and strange sounds and ghostly figures appear. 12 inches high. *From the Chris J. Russell and the Halloween Queen collection.*

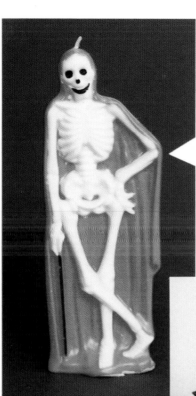

CANDLE, ca. 1965. Wax candle. 8.5 inches tall and made by Gurley of Buffalo, NY. *From the Hugh A. Luck collection.*

TEAPOT, ca. 1980. Witch and cauldron with bat spout. Teapots lend themselves to be made in whimsical shapes. Made in England. *From the Chris J. Russell and the Halloween Queen collection.*

SCULPTURE, ca. 1985. 5 inch high wood carving by folk artist Watkins.

PAINTING, 1984. An oil painting by S. Schneider of the space shuttle putting the witch in front of the moon for Halloween. 14.5 inches by 18 inches.

JEWELRY, 1988. Trick or Treat earrings each only .75 inches wide.

NEW YORKER, 1947. Magazine cover.

NEW YORKER, 1947. Magazine cover.

NEW YORKER, 1949. Magazine cover.

NEW YORKER, 1968. Magazine cover.

NEW YORKER, 1972. Magazine cover.

NEW YORKER, 1950. Magazine cover.

NEW YORKER, 1969. Magazine cover.

NEW YORKER, 1988. Magazine cover.

NEW YORKER, 1967. Magazine cover.

NEW YORKER, 1970. Magazine cover.

NEW YORKER, 1991. Magazine cover.

BOGIE BOOK, 1912. By Dennison.

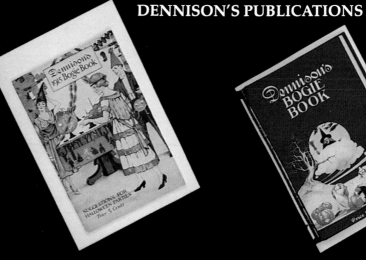

BOGIE BOOK, 1915. By Dennison.

BOGIE BOOK, 1920. By Dennison.

BOGIE BOOK, 1913. By Dennison.

BOGIE BOOK, 1916. By Dennison.

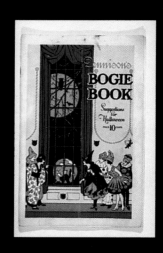

BOGIE BOOK, 1921. By Dennison.

BOGIE BOOK, 1914. By Dennison.

BOGIE BOOK, 1919. By Dennison with its mailing cover.

BOGIE BOOK, 1922. By Dennison.

BOGIE BOOK, 1926. By Dennison.

PARTIES MAGAZINE, 1929. By Dennison.

BOGIE BOOK, 1924. By Dennison.

PARTY MAGAZINE, 1927. By Dennison.

WHAT NEXT?, 1929. This was a Dennison fall season similar to the Bogie books.

BOGIE BOOK, 1925. By Dennison.

PARTY MAGAZINE, 1928. By Dennison.

NEW BOGIE BOOK, 1931. By Dennison.

HALLOWE'EN PARTIES, 1934. By Dennison.

MECHANICAL TOY, ca. 1910. "Pumpkin Head man", wood head, German-made, spring wound mechanism makes him get taller and then shorter. 8.5 inches tall. *From the Chris J. Russell and the Halloween Queen collection.*

games and toys

GAME, 1904. Sort of a Pin-the-Eyes-on-the-Pumpkin game. Printed on cloth by Saalfield Publishing, Ohio. Size is 18" x 28" and the numbers/eyes would have been cut out to play. *From the Chris J. Russell and the Halloween Queen collection.*

PARTY GAME, ca. 1916. Fortune Teller with all the attributes of a great item. It has superb lithography, is old, is in great condition and the graphics are wonderful. Each pumpkin would have been torn off and the fortune on its back read to the rest of the party. 18 inches across.

JACK IN THE BOX, ca. 1905. Paper-covered wooden box with composition heads, German-made, 6.5 inches tall. *From the Chris J. Russell and the Halloween Queen collection.*

PARTY GAME, ca. 1922. "Cat and Witch" was a Halloween version of pin the tail on the donkey. Made in USA by Whitman Publishing.

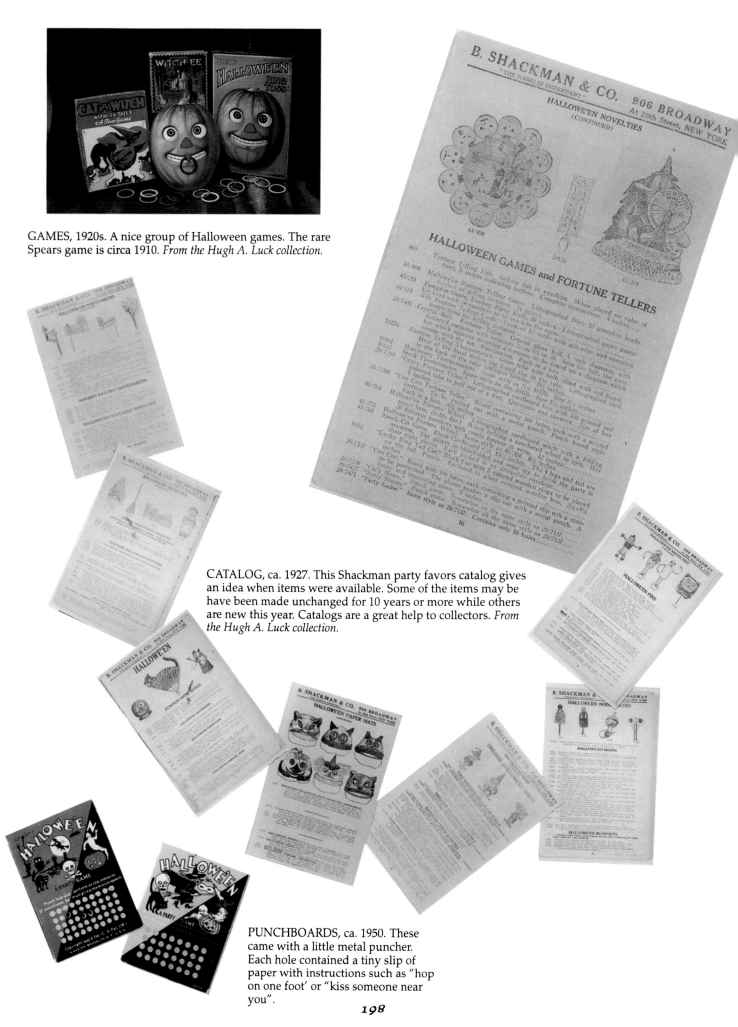

GAMES, 1920s. A nice group of Halloween games. The rare Spears game is circa 1910. *From the Hugh A. Luck collection.*

CATALOG, ca. 1927. This Shackman party favors catalog gives an idea when items were available. Some of the items may be have been made unchanged for 10 years or more while others are new this year. Catalogs are a great help to collectors. *From the Hugh A. Luck collection.*

PUNCHBOARDS, ca. 1950. These came with a little metal puncher. Each hole contained a tiny slip of paper with instructions such as "hop on one foot' or "kiss someone near you".

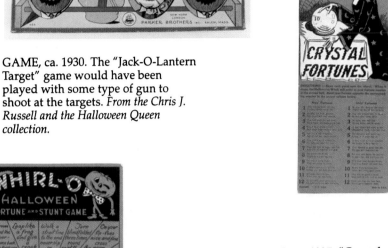

GAME, ca. 1930. The "Jack-O-Lantern Target" game would have been played with some type of gun to shoot at the targets. *From the Chris J. Russell and the Halloween Queen collection.*

PARTY GAMES, ca. 1940. "Jack-O-Lantern" told fortunes. Guests spun the wheel to learn their fate. "I'm A Dumbell" is a stunt game where one spun the wheel and had to do what the game called for. Made in USA. 12 inches tall.

GAME, ca. 1930. "Witch's Mystery Answer Game" made by Beistle. 12 inches tall. *From the Hugh A. Luck collection.*

PARTY GAME, ca. 1930. The "Whirl-O Halloween Fortune and Stunt Game" made one's guests do silly stunts such as "Throw ten feet never fail three potatoes in a pail". Guests spun the wheel to learn their fate. Made in USA by Beistle Co. 10 inches tall.

PARTY GAME, ca. 1927. "Crystal Fortunes" told fortunes. Guests spun the wheel to learn their fate. Made in USA by H.E. Luhrs. 12 inches tall.

SQUEEZE TOYS, ca. 1950. Hard plastic squeeze toys made in the USA by Fun World. Push in the button on the bottom and their arms and heads move. 3.5 inches tall. *From the Chris J. Russell and the Halloween Queen collection.*

TOY, ca. 1935. Rub the stick and the vibrations make the card and design spin. It didn't work for me.

GAME, ca. 1930. A lithographed cardboard bean bag toss game called "Goblo" and made in the USA. It is about 12 inches tall. *From the Hugh A. Luck collection.*

trick or treat bags

TRICK OR TREAT BAG, ca.1955. Another beautiful bag. It incorporates all the Halloween imagery: Witches, Jack-O'-Lanterns, black cats, and trick or treating. The bag is about 10 inches tall.

TRICK 'R TREAT BAG, ca. 1955. 12 inches tall, not including handle.

TRICK OR TREAT BAG, ca.1940. 14 inches tall, not including handle.

TRICK OR TREAT BAG, ca. 1959. Cat with bow tie image. 14 inches tall, not including handle.

TRICK 'R TREAT BAG, ca. 1955. 14 inches tall, not including handle.

TRICK OR TREAT BAG, ca. 1960. 14 inches tall, not including handle.

TRICK OR TREAT BAG, ca. 1948. An unusual Popeye's Trick or Treat bag. 14 inches tall not including handle.

TRICK OR TREAT BAG, ca.1955. The soft drink maker, Orange Crush, produced this bag. It incorporates typical Halloween imagery: Witches, bats, and trick or treating. The bag is about 10 inches tall.

TRICK OR TREAT BAG, ca. 1955. 14 inches tall, not including handle.

TRICK OR TREAT BAG, ca. 1960. 14 inches tall, not including handle.

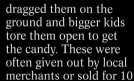

TRICK OR TREAT BAG, ca.1955. Trick or treat bags rarely survived. Little kids dragged them on the ground and bigger kids tore them open to get the candy. These were often given out by local merchants or sold for 10 cents. 18 inches tall.

TRICK OR TREAT BAG, ca.1960. When it comes to trick or treat bags, this one is a beauty. It shows a neighborhood scene with kids pulling pranks o the homeowners. One kid is even carrying the same bag in the scene. The bag is about 14 inches tall.

TRICK OR TREAT BAG, ca. 1959. 14 inches tall, not including handle

TRICK OR TREAT BAG, ca. 1960. Made for Howdy Beefburgers 18 inches tall, not including handle.

TRICK OR TREAT BAG, ca. 1964. Distributed by Esso 14 inches tall, not including handle.

TRICK OR TREAT BAG, ca. 1988. Witch and ghosts, made in Taiwan. 10.5 inches tall, not including handle.

TRICK OR TREAT BAG, ca. 1990. Haunted house, by Midwest Importers of Cannon Falls. 17 inches tall, not including handle.

TRICK OR TREAT BAG, ca. 1985. Cat on a fence, Hallmark. 13 inches tall, not including handle.

TRICK OR TREAT BAG, ca. 1990. Dancing skeletons, by Applause. Glows in the dark and is 13 inches tall, not including handle.

TRICK OR TREAT BAG, ca. 1990. Black cat, by Russ Berrie. 17 inches tall, not including handle.

TRICK OR TREAT BAG, ca. 1987. Smiling ghost, Hallmark. 13 inches tall, not including handle.

TRICK OR TREAT BAG, ca. 1990. Jack-O'-Lantern, by Goodman Fraser. 13 inches tall, not including handle.

TRICK OR TREAT BAG, ca.1960. A hard-to-find bag, since it was made of thermoformed plastic similar to a Halloween mask. The face of the bag is three-dimensional. The bag is about 10 inches tall.

TRICK OR TREAT BAG, ca. 1988. Cat and pumpkin, the Stephen Lawrence Co. 9.5 inches tall, not including handle.

TRICK OR TREAT BAGS, 1990. McDonalds put out this series of 3 bags. They glow in the dark and are made out of vinyl or heavy plastic. 12 inches tall not including handle.

COUNTRY HOUSE. This country home has decorations on the porch, but the eye catcher is the scarecrow horse, driver and dandy passenger.

YARD HAUNT, 2009. Decorating front yards for Halloween seems to grow more popular each year. This display is visited by hundreds of trick or treaters each year. The idea is to create a scary, but safe environment for kids to enjoy as they go from house to house begging for treats.

DECORATED YARDS. Cemeteries, ghosts, witches and ghosts can be elaborate or as simple as needed. The small touches, such as a hand sticking up from the ground or a monster with baby send shivers up the spine of the casual passer by.

DECORATED HOUSES. There are numerous ways to decorate for Halloween. Ghosts, gravestones, skeletons, cobwebs, Jack-O-Lanterns, etc. help to put the visitor on notice that Halloween is celebrated here.

parties

In the Roaring 20s, Halloween parties were the rage - card parties, town dances, social club gatherings, and more - and the variety of decorations followed suit. *Bogie Books* show parties with themes such as an Oriental Halloween or Halloween with an art deco flair to the costumes and decorations. By the 1930s, Halloween was being celebrated more by adults than by their children. Photos and publications of the periods give an indication of what was happening.

If you have a Halloween party, plan well in advance. Send out your invitations early and ask your guests to plan their costumes several weeks in advance. Try to have the party on the Saturday night before (or, luckily, on) Halloween. Presently, good decorating material is put out by Hallmark, American Greeting and others. For Halloween, the more decorations you use, the better the effect. Try orange and black crepe streamers. Buy extra plates, napkins and table covers as they may not be available the following year when they will also cost more. Save whatever you can and use it in the following year.

PHOTO, ca. 1925. A lovely luncheon Halloween party with costumes and decorations. *From the Chris J. Russell and the Halloween Queen collection.*

finally...pumpkin pie

In closing, let me offer you a Halloween pumpkin pie recipe that has been perfected over the past 20 years.

The very best Pumpkin Pie.
A simple recipe.

Ingredients:
One 16 ounce can of solid packed pumpkin. (If you use fresh pumpkin, it is a bit stringy and contains too much water unless dried out in the oven).
1/4 to 3/4 cup of sugar. This can be brown sugar or white. (White sugar is brown sugar with the molasses removed. Feel free to use less sugar and enjoy the low sugar dessert.
1/2 teaspoon of salt
1/2 teaspoon of baking soda
2 to 4 tablespoons of Molasses
1 teaspoon of ground cinnamon (more is not better)
1/4 teaspoon of ground cloves
1/4 teaspoon of ground nutmeg
1 to 1 1/2 teaspoons of grated fresh ginger. (Buy the ginger root and wrap it in a few baggies and store it in your freezer. It will last for many months.)
12 ounce can of evaporated milk plus 2 ounces of regular or skim milk
2 eggs
1 pre-made pie crust (These are available in your freezer or refrigerated section of the supermarket. They are quick and efficient) or make your own. I make a poor pie crust and I am the first to admit it.

Put all the ingredients in the bowl except the eggs and mix well. Beat the eggs gently in a separate bowl and then add to the main bowl. Mix gently. The object is to incorporate the eggs without overbeating them.

Preheat oven to 425 degrees, then when it is up to temperature, pour the mixture in the pie crust and put the pie in the center of the oven. After 15 minutes, lower the temperature to 350 degrees and cook for about 30 or 40 minutes or until a knife or toothpick inserted in the middle comes out clean.

That's it. Here is a tip to keep it tasting great. After it cools, cover it with Saran wrap and leave it on the counter. Do not refrigerate it. It will last for at least 4 days at room temperature. These pumpkin pies do not stay around that long unless we make 3 at a time.

BíBLíOGRAPhy

Dennison. *Bogie Books.*

Blain, Mary. *Games For Halloween*. Barse & Hopkins, 1912.

Simons, Evelyn. *Spooky Halloween Entertainments.* Ohio: Paine Publishing, 1923.

Schauffler, Robert Haven. *Hallowe'en.* New York: Dodd Mead & Co., New York, 1935.

Bannatyne, Lesley Pratt. *Halloween, An American Holiday, An American Experience.* New York: Facts On File, New York, 1990.

Resources

Trick or Treat Trader, C.J. Russell and the Halloween Queen, P.O. Box 499, Winchester, NH 03470. Occasional newsletter for Halloween collectors.

Jenny Tarrant, 10221 Squire Meadow #D, St. Louis, MO 62123. Offers old holiday decorations.

Dunbars Gallery, 76 Haven Street, Milford, MA 01757. Auction house for holiday collectibles.

Halloween In America, 2nd Edition ©2010

price guide

Using This Guide

The values listed represent, in the opinion of the author, what an item *which is in excellent condition* might be valued at by the knowledgeable collector. Pieces illustrated vary in condition from poor to mint but are priced as Excellent. The price paid for any particular item will naturally vary by geographical location, and will be also be affected by the eagerness of the buyer, willingness of the seller, whether purchased at a retail shop, antique show, or flea market.

Items with broken, missing, or non-stock replacement parts are worth less than the values listed. Rare or desirable items in excellent or mint condition or with their original box can be worth several times the values indicated. For more information about valuing items, refer to page 15 on Valuing Halloween Memorabilia.

Ultimately the price paid for any particular item depends on the buyer and seller. The author does not claim to be the final authority on prices and assumes no responsibility for financial loss or gain based on the use of this guide.

Position Codes

T = Top
C = Center
B = Bottom
R = Right
L = Left
T-B = Top to bottom

TL = Top Left
TC = Top Center
TR = Top Right
BL = Bottom Left
BC = Bottom Center
L-R = Left to Right

BR = Bottom Right
CL = Center left
CR = Center right
TLC = Top left center
TRC = Top right center
R-L = Right to Left

PG	POS.	VALUE
4		300-350
5		10-15
6	L - R	325-400, 200-275, 150-210, 45-65 (cat)
8		110-135
9		325-375
10		12-17
11	L	18-25
11	R	16-18 ea.
12		8-10
13		300-350
14		65 ea.
16		10-12 ea.
17		65-75
18	L	35-40
19	TL	6-8
19	TR	10-12
19	BR	55-65 ea.
20		300-325
21	L	125-200
21	R	8-12
22		30-35
23	R	12
24		8-20 ea.
25		10-20 ea.
26	T	8-10 ea.
26	CR	12-16
26	BL	25-30
26	BR	8-10
27	TL	8-10
27	CL	5-6
27	BL	5-6
27	TR	40-50 ea.
27	CR	40-50 ea
27	BR	450-500
28	TL (L-R)	55-65, 100-125
28	BL (L-R)	60-85, 95-150
28	TR	375-425
28	CR	200-250
29	CL	200-250
29	BL	200-250
29	TR	200-250
29	CR	200-250
30	TL	175-225
30	BL (L-R)	150-200, 65-95
30	TR	25-45
30	CR	110-145
30	BR	200-250
31	TL	250-300 ea.
31	BL	125-175
31	TR	90-115
31	CR	100-135
31	BR	400-450
32	TL	45-65
32	CL	75-125
32	C	75-125
32	TR	35-50
32	CR	175-250
32	BR	175-250
33	TL	20-25
33	CL	85-110 ea.
33	TR	150-200 ea.
33	CR	45-55 set
33	BR	200-250 ea.
34	TL	35-45
34	CL	45-55
34	BL	35-45
34	C	35-45
34	CB	35-45
34	TR	65-85
34	BR	35-45
35	TL	30-45
35	C	15-20
35	TR	35-45
35	B	50-65 ea.
36	TL	40-45
36	CL	30-35 ea.
36	TR	100-150
37	BR	90-120
37	T - B	85-95, 85-95, 12-20, 12-20
37	TR	30-40
38	B	25-35
39		95-145 ea.
40	TL	95-145
40	BL	95-145
40	TR	30-35
40	BR	8-12
41	T	25-35 ea.
42	L	55-65
42	R	85-115
44	TL	45-60
45	CL	25-30
46	T	10-15 ea.
47	TR	60-75
47	BR	8-10
48	L (T-B)	6-8, 6-8, 6-8,
48	BL	15-20
48	TR	6-10
48	BR	8-12
49	TL	25-30
49	TR	30-40
49	C	65-90
49	BL	8-10
49	CR	40-55
50	T (L-R)	30-40, 35-45, 50-75
50	BL	12-15
50	BR	5-8
52	hats	8-12
53	hats	8-12
54	TL	45-55 MIB
54	BL	8-12
55	TL	40-45
55	TC	45-55
55	TR	25-35
56	TL	10-15
56	BL	35-40
56	R	70-80
57	L	30-40
57	TR	25-30
57	BR	30-40
58	T	25-30 ea.
58	C	25-30 ea.
58	B	25-30 ea.
59		25-30 ea.
60	TL	25-30 ea.
60	CL	25-30 ea.
60	R	25-30 ea.
61	T	35-40 ea.
61	B	25-30 ea.
62		10-15 ea.
63		25-30 ea.
64	TL	15-20 ea.
64	CL	30-36 ea.
64	TR	18-24
64	B	25-30 ea.
65	T	25-30 ea.
65	TRC	25-30
65	B	20-25 ea.
66	TL	20-25 ea.
66	TR	20-25 ea.
66	BL	12-18 ea.
66	BR	22-30 ea.
67	TL	13-16
67	TR	clockwise: 115, 115, 85, 145
67	BL	60-70 ea.
67	BR	13-16
68	TL	17-20 ea.
68	TR	15-20 ea.
68	CL	185, 65
68	BR	65-75 ea.
68	BL	65-75
69	TL	75-95 ea.
69	TR	30-35 ea.
69	BL	65-75 ea.
69	BR	35-45 ea.
70	T	18-24 ea.
70	B	65-75 ea.
71	T	80-95 ea.
71	CR (T-B)	55, 40
71	CL (T-B)	135, 25
71	BR	35
72	TL (L-R)	60, 45
72	TR	80-100 ea.
72	CL	55-70 ea.
72	B	65-85 ea.
73	L	18-24 ea.
73	TR	25-30 ea.
74		12-15 ea.
75	T	10-12 ea.
75	C	90-130
75	B & R	4-6 ea.
76	TL	6-9 ea.
76	CR	6-8
76	BL	80-95 complete
76	BR	6-9 ea.
77	TL	25-35
77	TR	5-7
77	B	6-9 ea.
78	T	95-120
78	BL	30-35
78	BR	10-12 ea.
79	TL	10-12
79	TR	10-12 ea.
79	CL	5-8 ea.
79	B	6-9 ea.
80	TL	30-35
80	BL	30-35
80	CR	15-20
80	BR	6-8
81	T	20-25
81	CR	25-30 pack
81	BL	65-75
82	TR	2-4 ea.
82	BL	2-4 ea.
82	BR	2-4 ea.
83	TL	2-4 ea.
83	TR	18-20
83	BL	95-125
83	BR	65-75
84	T	75-80 ea.
84	C	65-75
84	B	65-75
85	T	65-75
85	CL	65-75
85	CR	65-75
85	B	65-75
86	TL	55-70
86	TR	65-75
86	BL	65-75
86	BR	25-35
87	TL	35-40
87	TR	65-75
87	CL	45-60
87	BR	65-75
88	TL	45-55
88	TR	65-75
88	CR	50-75
88	BL	65-75
89	TR	65-75
89	BL	15-20 per roll
89	BR	55-60
90		18-24 ea.
91	TL (L-R)	45, 65
91	TR	75-90
91	BL	425-475
91	BR	60-75
92	TL	55-65
92	TR	65-75
92	CL	65-75
92	CR	125-175
92	BL	65-75
93	TL	30-35
93	CR	65-75
93	CL	65-75
93	BR	65-75
94	T	6-8
94	B	155-190 ea.
95	TL	65-75
95	TR	10-15
95	BL	60-85
95	BR	60-65
96	TL	85-95
96	R & B	30-45 per set
97	T	30-40
97	C	55-65
97	B	25-35
97	TR	25-30
98	TL	75-95
98	TR	75-95
98	C	25-35
98	B	800-950
99	TL	135-175
99	TR	55-65
99	BL	55-65
99	BR	60-70
100	TL	45-50
100	CL	65-70 ea.
100	BL	75-85
100	R	40-55 ea.
101	TL	15-20
101	TR	30-40
101	BL	30-40
101	CR	35-50
101	BR	12-18
102		275-350
103		55-80 ea.
104	TL	95-115 ea.
104	TR	70-85 ea.
104	BR	40-50
104	BL	55-80 ea.
105	TL	35-45
105	TR	45-50
105	B	35-55 ea.
106		35-55 ea.
107	T	15-20
107	BL	30-35
107	BR	8-10
108	TL	35-45
108	TR	35-45
108	CR	30-40
108	BL	8-15
108	BR	20-30
109	TL	20-25
109	TR	55-65
109	C	35-45
109	BL	35-45
109	BR	15-25
110	TL	35-45
110	TR	35-45
110	C	45-55
110	BL	10-12
110	BR	35-40 ea.
111	TL	6-9 ea.
111	TR	6-9
111	CL	10-20
111	CB	28-35
111	BR	28-35
112		8-15 ea.
113		8-15 ea.
114	TL	45-60 ea.
114	TR	25-30
114	C	10-15 ea.
114	B	10-15
115	TL	25-30
115	TC	12-15
115	R & B	20-25 ea.
115	CL	25-30
116	T	1-2 per doz.
117	TL	500-650
117	TR	200-275 ea.
117	CR	500-650
117	B	850-1,000 ea.
118	TL	250-350
118	TR	475-525
118	CL	450-500
118	BL	600-700
118	BR	500-550
119	TL	450-525
119	TR	350-400
119	CL	350-400
119	BL	300-325
119	BC	125-155
119	BR	250-300
120	TR	85-110
120	CL	35-45
120	BR	45-65
121	T	45-65
121	BL	1,500-1,700
121	BR	450-525
122	TL	450-525
122	TR	450-600
122	CR	400-500
122	BL	300-400
122	BR	450-550
123	TL	450-500
123	TR	450-600 ea.
123	CL	125-225 ea.
123	CR	300-375
123	BL (L-R)	355, 275
123	BR	500-650
124	TL	225-265
124	TR	450-600
124	CL	175-250
124	BL	375-450

Page	Loc.	Value
124	BR	1250-1400
125	TL (L-R)	275-375, 1000-1100
125	CR	295-325
125	BL	45-60
125	BR	30-40
126	TL	55-75
126	TR	45-65
126	B	45-65 ea.
127	T	40-50 ea.
127	BL	375-450
127	BR	400-500
128	T (L-R)	145, 345, 155
128	B	45-60 ea.
129	TL	400-450 ea.
129	TR	500-600
129	BL	350-450
129	BR	125-175
130	TR	95-125
130	BL	300-350
130	BR	40-50
131	T	35-45 ea.
131	B	35-55 ea.
132	TL	65-200
132	TR	85-200
132	BL	125-350
132	BR	35-45
133	TL	265-300
133	TR	95-160
133	BL	40-55
133	BR	75-90
134	TL	50-70
134	CR	40-50 ea.
134	BL	40-50
135	CL	30-35
135	TR	95-135
135	BR	85-125 ea.
136	T	35-45 ea.
136	BL	550-650
136	BR	300-350
137	TL	650-750
137	TR (L-R)	300-375, 365-450
137	CL	550-650
137	BL	350-450
137	BR	350-425
137	MR	325-350 ea.
138	TL	145-165
138	TR	75-100
138	CL	2,000-2,500
138	BC	450-550
138	BR	600-650
139	TL	850-1,200
139	TR	35-45 ea.
139	CL	425-500
139	C	450-550 ea.
139	CR	475-525
139	BR	400-500
140	TL	175-300 ea., 85
140	TR	550-650
140	BL	375-400 ea.
140	BR	150-200
141	TL	350-400
141	TR (L-R)	350-550, 300-350
141	BL	125-130
141	BR	375-425
142	TL	350-400
142	TR	165-225
142	TCL	100-120
142	CL	125-155
142	BCL	250-275
142	BR	150-175
142	B	175-200
143	TL (L-R)	325-350, 375-400
143	TR	750-800
143	BL	650-700
143	BR	95-125
144	TL	375-425
144	TC (L-R)	275-300, 80-90
144	TR	240-275 ea.
144	BL	285-335
144	BC	450-550
144	BR	450-575
145	TL	70-85
145	TC	400-550
145	TR	250-300
145	BL	450-500
145	BC	275-300
145	BR (L-R)	275-350, 450-550
146	TL	350-425
146	TC	150-175
146	TR	360-385 ea.
146	BL	175-195 ea.
146	BC	300-325
146	BR	300-375
147	TL	300-325
147	TC	175-195
147	TR	450-650 ea.
147	BL	450-650
147	BC	350-425
147	BR (L-R)	425-450, 450-500
148	TL	275-300
148	TCL	245-275 ea.
148	TCR	250-300
148	TR	450-550
148	BL	250-275
148	BCL	600-800
148	BR	175-200
149	TL (L-R)	235-270, 350-385
149	TR	400-550 ea.
149	BL (L-R)	275-350, 250-300
149	BC	350-400
149	BR	385-425 ea.
150	TL	400-500
150	CL	400-450 ea.
150	CR	245-275
150	BL (L-R)	350-500, 275-300
150	BR	750-900
151	TL	250-275
151	TR	2,500-3,000
151	BL	800-950
151	BR	150-200 ea.
152	TL	185-225
152	TC	65-85
152	TR	450-600
152	BL	300-325 big, 95-150 small
153	TL	250-275
153	TC (L-R)	80-110, 70-90
153	TR	75-100
153	BL	850-1,000
153	BR	750-850
154	TL (L-R)	300-350, 450-500
154	TR	75-125
154	CL	225-300 ea.
154	BL (L-R)	375-425, 85-125
154	BR	350-450
155	TL	250-325 ea.
155	TR	225-300 ea.
155	BL	550-625
155	BC	400-525
155	BR	350-375
156	TL	400-475
156	TC	175-250
156	BL	475-525
156	BC	450-500
156	BR	550-650
157	TL	135-175
157	TR	250-350
157	BL	300-350
157	BR	600-700
158	TL	950-1050
158	TR	375-475
158	CL	400-450
158	BC	425-550
158	BR	450-500
159	TL (L-R)	350-400, 240-300
159	TR	325-375 ea.
159	BL	200-250
159	BC	155-200
159	BR	450-550
160	TL (L-R)	400-500, 325-350
160	TR	375-450
160	BL	600-700
160	CR	300-350
160	BR	400-450
161	TL	185-250 ea.
161	TR	185-250 ea.
161	C	45-65
161	B	225-300 ea.
162	TL	275-325
162	TC (L-R)	325-375, 275-325
162	CR	100-150
162	CL	60-90 ea.
162	BR	85-110
163	TL	350-400
163	TR	55-75 ea.
163	CR	300-400
163	BL	300-370
163	BR	50-75 ea.
164	TL	300-370
164	TC	200-250
164	CR	75-95 ea.
164	B	225-275 ea.
165	TL	50-75
165	TR	275-325
165	C	125-145
165	B	200-275 ea.
166	TL	130-150
166	TR (L-R)	200-225, 200-225
166	BL	50-75
166	BR	200-275
167	TL	350-400
167	TR	350-395 ea.
167	B	200-250
168	TL (T-B)	200-225, 100-135
168	BR (L-R)	40-45, 200-225
169	TL (L-R)	125-145, 85-95
169	TC	125-175
169	CR	125-175
169	BL	95-125
169	BC	35-40
169	BR	175-225
170	TR	35-50
170	CL	350-375
170	BR	35-50
170	BL	65-90
171	TL	50-70
171	TR	30-40 ea.
171	BL (L-R)	55-95, 90-160
171	CR	40-45
171	BR	45-55
172	TL	18-20
172	TR	55-175 ea.
172	BL	475-525
172	BR	150-175
173	TL	30-35
173	TR	1200
173	CL	175-225
173	BL	125-150
173	BR	35-45 ea.
174	TL	6-8
174	TR	35-45
174	BR	75-95
175	TL	35-45
175	TR	20-25
175	BL	35-45
175	BR	12-16
176	TL	75-95
176	TR	50-75
176	BL	12-16
176	BR	15-20
177	TL	25-35
177	TR	6-10
177	BL	10-14
177	BR	450-500
178	TL	75-95
178	TC	175-200
178	TR	40-55 ea.
178	CR	20-25 ea.
178	BL	40-55 ea.
178	BR	65-90
179	TL	75-110 ea.
179	TR	95-125
179	BL	65-95 ea.
179	BR	65-95 ea.
180	TL	7-10
180	TR	175-250
180	CR	20-25
180	BL	20-40 ea.
181	TL	40-45
181	TR	275-425 the set
181	CR	20-25
181	B	55-65 ea.
182	TL	85-100
182	TR	150-175
182	BL	6-8
182	BC	7-10
182	BR	90-115
183	TL	95-125
183	TR	40-45
183	BL	50-55
183	BR	45-55
184	T	75-85
184	L	95-125
184	CR	10-15
184	BR	125-150
185	TR	5-10
185	B	10-15 ea.
186	TL	75-85
186	C	35-45 ea.
186	BL	300-400
186	BR	165 full display
187	TL	6-8
187	TR	15-20
187	BL	30-40
187	BR	10-15
188	TL	12-15
188	TR	5-8
188	BL	30-45
188	BR	30-45
189	TR	25-30
189	CL	30-45 ea.
191	TL	85-130
191	BR	500-600
192	TL	15-20
192	TR	95-125
192	CL	100-150
192	B	6-9
193		25-30
194		12-30 ea.
195		65-160 ea.
196		65-135 ea.
197	TL	20
197	TR	450-500
197	CL	80-100
197	CR	245-290
197	BL	185-225 ea.
197	BR	40-45
198	TL	45-175
198	BL	8-12
199	TL	25-35 ea.
199	TC	125-145
199	TR	25-35
199	CL	35-45
199	C	30-40
199	BL	85-135
199	BC	25-35
199	BR	35-40 ea.
200	TCL	25-30
200	MCL	18-24
200	BCL	25-30
200	L (T-B)	45, 85, 25
200	C (T-B)	25, 30, 25, 20
200	R (T-B)	30, 20, 25, 20
201	L (T-B)	20, 10, 8, 8
201	C (T-B)	8, 12, 12, 6
201	CR	25-30
201	R (T-B)	8, 8, 6, 6

index